CONTENTS

Hi there square eyes! First, let's thank Philo T. Farnsworth and Vladimir Zworykin for developing the television set. Without it I would most likely have had no childhood, no business and no career in games.

During my childhood, I couldn't get enough of old TV reruns. My days started at six in the morning with *The Lone Ranger* and *The Rifleman*. At lunch, I would rush home to see *My Little Margie* and after school I would dream of flying as I watched *Superman*, starring George Reeves. Television taught me popular culture, history, geography and science. It allowed me to travel around the world with Alexander Munday and to "Utopian" towns like Mayberry, Mayfield and Hooterville.

I liked TV in the 1960s and all of my friends counted on me to let them know what the cool shows were. In the '70s and '80s, my interest in trivia and games was largely fueled by my love of television.

Now, 30 years later, I live in San Francisco and am raising three daughters with my wife. They think TV is too violent and don't appreciate a good gunfight in *Bonanza* or a classic drug bust on *Starsky and Hutch*.

But that's OK, I didn't create *Ultimate TV Trivia*™ for them anyway. I wrote it for you and your friends. This book is designed to invite conversation and rattle your memory. I hope that you laugh at some of the questions and argue about some of the answers. Enjoy this book and drop me a line if I hit a nerve, or if there's a Blankety Blank that you just can't remember.

Bob

RULES

For 1 or more players!

OBJECT

Put your TV knowledge to good use while collecting points. Be the first to collect 15 points and win the master couch potato crown!

CATEGORIES

✺ **Who Said That?**   Identify quotes from TV characters and theme songs

✺ **Where Did It Happen?**   Match characters and TV shows to their locations

   Blankety Blanks?   Fill in the blanks

✺ **TV Life/Real Life**   Answer questions about your favorite stars and the gossip – both on and off the screen.

PLAYING THE GAME

- First things first: grab a pen and paper to keep score and flip to page 10 (or where you left off last time).
- The player whose birthday is the closest to July 1 gets to be the first **Controller**. (The FCC declared July 1, 1941 the official start of commercial television in the US.) The **Controller** spins the spinner and asks the player to his/her left to answer a question from the category selected.

- *If the player guesses correctly*, s/he gets a point and play continues in a clockwise direction.
- *If the player guesses incorrectly*, play continues in a clockwise direction. There is no penalty for an incorrect response. However, if playing with three or more players, the next player can try to answer the previous player's question and then his/her own from the next category on the page. If successful, that player gets 2 points.
- Play continues in a clockwise direction with the **Controller** reading the next player a question from the next category on the page until *all four questions are asked*. (If the first question was from TV Life/Real Life, the next question is from Who Said That?)
- Don't worry if one player gets the opportunity to answer more than one question – the advantage will shift with each spin!
- After all of the questions have been attempted, the person to the **Controller's** left becomes the new **Controller**. S/he takes a spin and play continues.

WINNING THE GAME

- The first player to collect 15 points is the winner!

PLAYING ON YOUR OWN

- Grab a TV dinner, give yourself 20 minutes on the clock and take a spin! Start with the category on which the spinner lands and then move to the one below. Try to answer all four questions and give yourself one point for every question you get right. If you answer all of the questions on the page correctly, a bonus point is awarded. If you score more than 20 points in 20 minutes, you win. Too easy? Try to do it in 15 minutes or less.
- If you guess correctly, give yourself a point and spin again. If you guess incorrectly, take away a point. If you have no points, simply continue playing.
- Collect 20 points in twenty minutes or less and you're a winner!

Ultimate TV Trivia™

Which Golden Girl said, "I don't like him. I can't put my finger on it, but if I did, I'd have to wash it": Sophia, Rose or Blanche?

Major Nelson takes Jeannie to which state after finding her on a deserted island?

The sitcom _____ _____ is an adaptation of the British comedy *Man about the House*.

When Brandy's real-life brother joined the cast of *Moesha*, how was his character Dorian related to Moesha?

Answers: ✷ Sophia ✷ Florida (*I Dream of Jeannie*) ✷ *Three's Company* ✷ He is her cousin. (It is later revealed he is her half-brother.)

Ultimate TV Trivia

On *Survivor*, who says, "The tribe has spoken": Jeff Probst, Richard Hatch or Tina Wesson?

Where in New York City did Arnold and Willis Jackson live before moving into Mr. Drummond's Park Avenue penthouse?

Mork and Mindy was created as a spin-off of _____ _____ after Robin Williams' character Mork made two popular appearances on the show.

What is the fictional relationship of Kip and Henry to Buffy and Hildy in the '80s sitcom *Bosom Buddies*?

Answers: ❖ Jeff Probst ❖ Harlem (*Diff'rent Strokes*) *Happy Days* ❖ They are their brothers. (They are also the same people.)

Ultimate TV Trivia

Who Said That?

Who on *Will & Grace* said, "Oh Lorraine (played by Minnie Driver), who ever told you that you could pull off a leather jumpsuit": Will, Grace or Karen?

_____

Where Did It Happen?

Does Balki Bartokomous of *Perfect Strangers* hail from the country of Bartock, Ork or Mypos?

_____

Blankety Blanks

The working title of _____ ____ _____ before its 1987 premiere was *Not the Cosbys*.

_____

TV Life Real Life

South Park's Kyle and Ike are brothers, but not the same nationality. In what country was Ike born?

Answers: ❖ Karen ❖ Mypos ❖ *Married. . . with Children* ❖ Canada

Ultimate TV Trivia™

What phrase does Steve Urkel of *Family Matters* often utter?

From what city does the *S.S. Minnow* set sail before getting stranded on *Gilligan's Island*?

At the end of the *Knots Landing* series, mystery man Nigel tries to blow up Senator Greg Sumner's _____.

Which of these famous women has Scott Baio, the star of *Charles in Charge*, never actually dated: Pamela Anderson, Paula Abdul, Heather Locklear or Brooke Shields?

Ultimate TV Trivia

Who said, "People tell me I look like Ellen Degeneres": Christena Ferran (*Who Wants to Marry My Dad*), Carson Kressley (*Queer Eye for the Straight Guy*) or Jessica Simpson (*Newlyweds*)?

Brandon and Brenda Walsh moved from which midwestern state before calling Beverly Hills their home?

The Brady Bunch kids attend _____ High School.

How is Esther related to Fred Sanford on *Sanford and Son*?

Answers: ❖ Carson Kressley ❖ Minnesota ❖ Westdale ❖ She is his sister-in-law.

ULTIMATE

TV

Trivia™

Warning: Small parts may be a choking hazard. Not for children under 3 years.

ACKNOWLEDGMENTS

Editorial Director: Erin Conley

Designer: Michelle Hill

Special thanks to Suzanne Cracraft, Maria Llull, Cherie Martorana, Hillary Osness, Sabrina Reese
and Kristen Schoen who worked so hard (and fast) on this project.

© 2005 Bob Moog and University Games Corporation

First edition published in 2005

Spinner Books, a division of

University Games Corporation
2030 Harrison Street San Francisco CA 94110

University Games Europe B.V.
Australielaan 52 6199 AA Maastricht Airport Netherlands

University Games Australia
10 Apollo Street Warriewood 2102 Australia

Library of Congress Cataloging-in-Publication Data on file with the publisher.

ISBN 1-57528-968-7

Printed in China

1 2 3 4 5 6 7 8 9 10 - 09 08 07 06 05

ULTIMATE TV Trivia™

spinner books

San Francisco • Maastricht • Sydney

Ultimate TV Trivia

Which nerd said, "We had a meeting at the debate club that ran a little long. Kept arguing over what time to stop": Carol Seaver (*Growing Pains*), Alex P. Keaton (*Family Ties*) or Screech (*Saved by the Bell*)?

___ ___ ___ ___ ___

The O.C. takes place in which California beach town?

___ ___ ___ ___ ___

Fill in the blank to these *Fresh Prince of Bel-Air* theme song lyrics by Will Smith, "In West Philadelphia _____ ____ _____."

___ ___ ___ ___ ___

Tim O'Hara of *My Favorite Martian* refers to his Martian as what relation to disguise his true origin?

Ultimate TV Trivia

 Which child actor said, "Whatchoo talkin' 'bout?" on each show: Fred Savage, Gary Coleman or David Cassidy?

—————

 Name the two European cities where MTV's *The Real World* has taken place.

—————

 Leo Wyatt, husband of witch Piper on *Charmed*, is a _____ _____.

—————

 Which member of *3rd Rock from the Sun*'s Solomon family is the security officer and second-in-command when in alien form: Sally, Dick or Harry?

Answers: ❖ Gary Coleman (as Arnold Jackson on *Diff'rent Strokes*) ❖ London and Paris ❖ White lighter ❖ Sally

Ultimate TV Trivia™

Which *Married... with Children* character said, "They will never buy the cow if they can get the eggs for free": Kelly, Al or Peggy Bundy?

Where did Kotter of *Welcome Back, Kotter* attend high school: Buchanan High, Delta High or Lincoln High?

In order to win the _____-dollar prize, the ultimate "Survivor" must outplay the other contestants.

How many children do John and Olivia Walton of *The Waltons* have?

Ultimate TV Trivia

Who on *Happy Days* sings, "I found my thrill on Blueberry Hill": Chachi Arcola, Fonzie or Richie Cunningham?

_ . _ . _ . _ . _ . _ . _

On *That '70s Show,* where in Mexico did Laurie spend her honeymoon alone?

_ . _ . _ . _ . _ . _ . _

The names of the bachelors in the first three seasons of *The Bachelor* all begin with the letter ___.

_ . _ . _ . _ . _ . _ . _

On which '70s TV show does cousin Oliver join a TV family: *The Beverly Hillbillies*, *The Brady Bunch* or *The Partridge Family*?

Answers: ❧ Richie Cunningham ❧ Cancun ❧ A (Alex, Aaron, Andrew) ❧ *The Brady Bunch*

Ultimate TV Trivia™

Who on *The Brady Bunch* said, "Mom always says not to play ball in the house": Bobby, Peter or Jan Brady?

In what country did the show *Iron Chef* originate?

The boy band _____ was created on the first season of MTV's *Making the Band*.

Which actress plays neither a wife nor a lover of Blake Carrington on *Dynasty*: Heather Locklear, Joan Collins or Linda Evans?

Ultimate TV Trivia™

Which *All in the Family* character said, "I just thank God I'm an atheist": Archie Bunker, Mike Stivic or Gloria Stivic?

--- · --- · --- · --- · ---

Where is the Batpole, which leads to the Batcave, located?

--- · --- · --- · --- · ---

Showtime, the network that premiered *Queer as Folk*, unveiled a similar series called *The ___ _____*, with a female focus.

--- · --- · --- · --- · ---

What is the name of Gomer Pyle's cousin on *The Andy Griffith Show*: Gopher, Goober or Gipper?

Ultimate TV Trivia

Which *That '70s Show* character prayed, "Dear God, thank you so much for helping me quit such a filthy, disgusting, soothing, delicious habit": Kelso, Fez or Kitty?

_____

On *Happy Days*, the Cunningham family lives in what US city?

_____

Fill in the blanks for this *Brady Bunch* theme song: "… all of them had _____ of _____, like their mother."

_____

What is the name of Barney and Betty Rubble's son on *The Flintstones*?

Ultimate TV Trivia™

Who on *Happy Days* says, "You're such a Potsie": Fonzie, Ralph Malph or Richie?

———————

On *Sanford and Son*, junk dealers Fred and Lamont Sanford live in what city?

———————

Della Street works as a _____ on *Perry Mason*.

———————

On the western *Maverick*, what is the relationship between Bret and Bart Maverick?

Answers: ❖ Ralph Malph ❖ Los Angeles ❖ Secretary ❖ They are brothers.

Ultimate TV Trivia™

Which *Melrose Place* guy said, "Why is it that every time a girl doesn't show up at night, people think she's at my apartment": Jake Hanson, Dr. Michael Mancini or Dr. Peter Burns?

— — — — — — — — — —

What mountain range did the Beverly Hillbillies call home before moving to Beverly Hills?

— — — — — — — — — —

Andy and Opie Taylor of *The Andy Griffith Show* live in _____, North Carolina.

— — — — — — — — — —

Name the two Tuscadero sisters on *Happy Days*.

Answers: ❖ Jake Hanson ❖ Ozarks ❖ Mayberry ❖ Pinky and Leather

Ultimate TV Trivia™

Who on *The Sopranos* said, "Do you know any other garbage men who live in a house like this": Meadow Soprano, Tony Soprano or Christopher Moltisanti?

_ . _ . _ . _ . _ . _ . _

In what Ohio city does the Cleaver family of *Leave It to Beaver* live?

_ . _ . _ . _ . _ . _ . _

B.J. on *B.J. and the Bear* works as a _____.

_ . _ . _ . _ . _ . _ . _

Mailman Cliff Clavin of *Cheers* lives with which of his relatives?

Answers: ❖ Meadow Soprano ❖ Mayfield ❖ Trucker ❖ His mother

Ultimate TV Trivia™

After every broadcast, which news anchor said, "… and that's the way it is": David Brinkley, Walter Cronkite or Chet Huntley?

Where in Maine does Jessica Fletcher from *Murder She Wrote* reside?

The original roommates on *Three's Company* are Jack, Janet and _____.

Hank Hill of *King of the Hill* has two women in his life: Betsy and his wife, Peggy. Who is Betsy?

Answers: ❖ Walter Cronkite ❖ Cabot Cove ❖ Chrissy ❖ His guitar

Ultimate TV Trivia

Who on *The Simpsons* said, "Remember, you can always find east by staring at the sun": Bart Simpson, Homer Simpson or Krusty the Clown?

_ _ _ _ _ _ _ _ _

Which scary TV family lives at 1313 Mockingbird Lane?

_ _ _ _ _ _ _ _ _

The daytime duo _____ and _____ put their names together to create the Relly Awards.

_ _ _ _ _ _ _ _ _

What daytime talk show host is married to Connie Chung?

Ultimate TV Trivia™

Which *NYPD Blue* character said, "You got a lot of morons in your family? 'Cause that could be genetic": Detective Danny Sorenson, Detective Andy Sipowicz or Lieutenant Arthur Fancy?

What is the name of the company where the four business-women in *Designing Women* work?

"_____ gets a _____" is a phrase used on *Hollywood Squares*.

Which *Full House* sister had a best friend named Kimmy: DJ, Stephanie or Michelle?

Ultimate TV Trivia

Who Said That?

Who on *The Nanny* said, "Trust me, the only man who can satisfy a woman in two minutes is Colonel Sanders": Niles, Fran or Sylvia?

Where Did It Happen?

In what nutty grove do the adventures on *Little House on the Prairie* take place?

Blankety Blanks

Prince Adam is able to transform himself into He-Man when he holds the sword of power and utters the words "By the power of _____."

TV Life Real Life

Is Uncle Fester the uncle of Morticia Addams, Gomez Addams or Lily Munster?

Answers: ✣ Sylvia ✣ Walnut Grove ✣ Grayskull ✣ Morticia Addams (*The Addams Family*)

Ultimate TV Trivia

What TV dame said to one of her guests, "Are you nervous? Good": Sharon Osbourne, Judge Judy or Diane Sawyer?

_._._._._._

Which college does Joey of *Dawson's Creek* attend?

_._._._._._

_____ is the cable network whose programming includes almost 24 hours of soap opera reruns.

_._._._._._

Which show begins and ends each episode (except the last one) with a man telling a joke to his wife: *B.J. and the Bear*, *Welcome Back, Kotter* or *The Bob Newhart Show*?

Answers: ✲ Judge Judy ✲ Worthington ✲ SOAPnet ✲ *Welcome Back, Kotter* (In the last episode, he tells the joke to a stuffed bear.)

Ultimate TV Trivia™

Who said, "I've decided to catch a Heffalump": The Cat in the Hat™, Winnie-the-Pooh™ or Smurfette?

--- --- --- ---

Where do Yogi Bear and Boo Boo reside?

--- --- --- ---

Fill in the blanks to this theme song, "Teenage Mutant Ninja Turtles, _____ in a _____, Turtle power!"

--- --- --- ---

On *Dallas*, how is Gary Ewing related to J.R. Ewing?

Ultimate TV Trivia™

Who says, "Sufferin' succotash": Yosemite Sam, Sylvester the Cat or Daffy Duck?

_ _ _ _ _ _ _ _ _

Where do cartoon buddies Cartman and Kenny live?

_ _ _ _ _ _ _ _ _

On the '90s sitcom _Blossom_, the teenage main character had a best friend named after the number ____.

_ _ _ _ _ _ _ _ _

What family lives next door to Archie Bunker of _All in the Family_ until they move uptown?

Answers: ✷ Sylvester the Cat ✷ South Park ✷ Six (Le Muere) ✷ The Jeffersons

Ultimate TV Trivia™

 Who said, "I was the kind nobody thought could make it. I had a funny Boston accent. I couldn't pronounce my R's": Diane Sawyer, Tom Brokaw or Barbara Walters?

—————

 On *Dallas*, what is the name of the Ewing's sprawling ranch located just outside of Dallas, Texas?

—————

 During the first season of 7ᵗʰ *Heaven*, there were _____ Camden kids.

—————

 Name three of Shirley's five kids on *The Partridge Family*.

Answers: ❖ Barbara Walters ❖ South Fork ❖ Five (Twin boys were born later.) ❖ Keith, Laurie, Danny, Chris, Tracy

Ultimate TV Trivia

Which *Cheers* character said, "It's a dog-eat-dog world and I'm wearing Milk Bone underwear": Norm, Cliff or Woody?

———————————

In what city does the action of *Boomtown* take place?

———————————

JAG stands for _____ Advocate General.

———————————

On *Family Affair*, how is Bill Davis related to Cissy, Buffy and Jody?

Answers: ❖ Norm ❖ Los Angeles ❖ Judge ❖ He is their uncle.

Ultimate TV Trivia

Which *One Life to Live* villain said, "They say revenge is sweet. I'm about to go into sugar shock": Todd Manning, Dorian Lord or Lindsay Rappaport?

———————————

In *Spin City*, Michael J. Fox and Charlie Sheen take turns playing deputy mayor of what city?

———————————

Just Shoot Me takes place in the New York editorial offices of _____, a fictitious fashion magazine.

———————————

What is the name of Phoebe's twin sister on *Friends*?

Answers: ❖ Todd Manning ❖ New York City ❖ "Blush" ❖ Ursula (She got her start as a waitress on *Mad About You*.)

❖ 34 ❖

Ultimate TV Trivia™

Which *Star Trek* officer says, "Space, the final frontier": Captain Kirk, Commander Spock or "Bones" McCoy?

James Cameron's *Dark Angel* takes place in a post-apocalyptic version of what US city?

On the popular '70s series *Starsky and Hutch*, the two detectives frequently rely on a snitch nicknamed Huggy ____.

What is Ally's relationship to Billy on *Ally McBeal*?

Answers: ❖ Captain Kirk ❖ Seattle ❖ Bear ❖ They are childhood sweethearts and co-workers.

Ultimate TV Trivia

Which show describes itself as "A disturbingly perfect new drama": *The O.C.*, *Nip/Tuck* or *Las Vegas*?

_ _ _ _ _ _ _ _

On *The Mary Tyler Moore Show*, Mary works for a TV newsroom in what US city?

_ _ _ _ _ _ _ _

On *The Muppet Show*, Beaker is the assistant to Dr. _____.

_ _ _ _ _ _ _ _

What do members of the undercover A-Team have in common?

Ultimate TV Trivia

On what show does a secret agent listen to a recorded message that ends with the sentence, "This tape will self-destruct in five seconds"?

———————————

The '70s crime drama *The Rockford Files* takes place in what US city?

———————————

Fill in the remaining three words to this line from the TV theme song to *Green Acres*, "Green Acres is the _____ ___ ___."

———————————

How many children did The Huxtables have on *The Cosby Show*?

Ultimate TV Trivia™

Who says, "One of these days, Alice…": Ralph (*The Honeymooners*), Mel (*Alice*) or George (*The Jeffersons*)?

_._._._._._._._._

What planet is Mork on *Mork & Mindy* from?

_._._._._._._._._

In the '70s series *Land of the Lost*, the Marshall family is enjoying a _____ trip when an earthquake causes them to travel back into the time of dinosaurs.

_._._._._._._._._

Which relative often appears with Steve Irwin, the *Crocodile Hunter*, on his TV series?

Answers: ❖ Ralph Kramden ❖ Ork ❖ Rafting ❖ His wife (Terri)

Ultimate TV Trivia

Which *Taxi* character said, "I'm not really a cab driver. I'm just waiting for something better to come along. You know, like death": Alex Rieger, Elaine Nardo or Jeff Bennett?

— — — — — — — —

The TV series *M*A*S*H* is set in what country?

— — — — — — — —

On *The Odd Couple*, Oscar Madison makes his living as a

_____ _____.

— — — — — — — —

Sally Field made guest appearances on what medical drama as Abby Lockhart's bipolar mother?

Ultimate TV Trivia

Which *Happy Days* personality said, "Here, have a LifeSaver®, it'll make you feel better": Howard Cunningham, Fonzie or Joanie Cunningham?

———————

Detective Robert T. Ironside battles the bad guys while sitting where?

———————

On the popular series *M*A*S*H*, the letters stand for:
M_____ A_____ S_____ H_____.

———————

Name the historic '50s variety show that featured Sid Caesar, Carl Reiner and Imogene Coca, with famous writers including Mel Brooks, Woody Allen and Neil Simon.

Answers: ❖ Howard Cunningham ❖ In a wheelchair (*Ironside*) ❖ Mobile Army Surgical Hospital ❖ *Your Show of Shows*

Ultimate TV Trivia™

Who often says, "Dy-no-mite": J.J. (*Good Times*), Rerun (*What's Happening!!*) or Willis (*Diff'rent Strokes*)?

On the classic show *Get Smart*, where is Agent Maxwell Smart's phone hidden?

Fill in the blanks to the *The Partridge Family* theme song, "Hello, world, hear the song that we're singing, _____ _____ _____!"

Which *Golden Girls* character is Sophia's daughter: Blanche, Rose or Dorothy?

Ultimate TV Trivia

Who on *Mary Tyler Moore* said, "You know you got spunk! ... I hate spunk": Lou Grant, Mary Richards or Ted Baxter?

. _ . _ . _ . _ . _

On the '70s comedy *Green Acres*, Oliver Wendell Douglas and his wife, Lisa, move from New York to what rural community?

. _ . _ . _ . _ . _

News personality _____ _____ underwent a live televised colonoscopy in 2000.

. _ . _ . _ . _ . _

What is the full name of George Burns' wife, who starred with him on a TV show bearing both their names?

Answers: Lou Grant ❖ Hooterville ❖ Katie Couric ❖ Gracie Allen

Ultimate TV Trivia

Who says, "Kiss my grits": Flo (*Alice*), Daisy Duke (*Dukes of Hazzard*) or Aunt Clara (*Bewitched*)?

Was Rhoda Morgenstern Gerard of the '70s show *Rhoda* born in The Bronx, Brooklyn or Queens?

From 1967 through 1992, _____ _____ was the bandleader for *The Tonight Show* starring Johnny Carson.

Teen heartthrobs Parker Stevenson and Shaun Cassidy play brothers in what '70s mystery series?

Ultimate TV Trivia

Who says, "Well, doggies": Jed Clampett (*The Beverly Hillbillies*), Sheriff Rosco P. Coltrane (*Dukes of Hazzard*) or Fred Sanford (*Sanford and Son*)?

What TV family lives on 000 Cemetery Lane?

Fill in the blank to this popular quote by Arthur "Big Guy" Carlson from the '70s sitcom *WKRP in Cincinnati*, "As _____ is my witness, I thought _____ could fly."

What is the name of the family that befriends Harry, a Bigfoot-type beast, and invites him into their home?

Ultimate TV Trivia™

On which soap opera did Erica yell, "You can't hurt me! I'm Erica Kane!" when a bear was about to attack: *Days of Our Lives, All My Children* or *General Hospital?*

On *The Facts of Life*, at what school does Edna Garrett guide Tootie, Blair, Jo and Natalie?

_____ _____ works as an anchor man at the television newsroom with Mary on *The Mary Tyler Moore Show*.

Who is the youngest angel on *Touched by An Angel*: Tess (Della Resse), Gloria (Valerie Bertinelli) or Monica (Roma Downey)?

Answers: ❖ *All My Children* ❖ The Eastland School for Girls ❖ Ted Baxter (played by Ted Knight) ❖ Gloria

Ultimate TV Trivia

Who Said That?

On what show can the greeting, "Hey, hey, hey" be heard: *What's Happening!!*, *The Carol Burnett Show* or *Good Times*?

_ _ _ _ _ _ _ _ _ _

Where Did It Happen?

Jon and Ponch of *CHiPs* cruise the highways in and around what west coast city?

_ _ _ _ _ _ _ _ _ _

Blankety Blanks

Fill in the blanks to Chevy Chase's opening line from the "Weekend Update" on *Saturday Night Live*, "Good Evening, I'm Chevy Chase, and _____ ____."

_ _ _ _ _ _ _ _ _ _

TV Life Real Life

On *Hope and Faith*, is Hope the suburban mom or the former soap star?

Answers: ☆ *What's Happening!!* ☆ Los Angeles ☆ You're not ☆ The suburban mom

Ultimate TV Trivia

On what cartoon might you hear the quote, "Charmander char char": *Teenage Mutant Ninja Turtles*, *Tales from the Crypt* or *Pokémon*?

—————————————

On *Welcome Back, Kotter*, Mr. Kotter lives and teaches at his old alma mater in what New York borough?

—————————————

Fill in the blanks to the theme song from *The Monkees*: "Here we come, walkin' down the street. We get the _____ _____ from Ev'ry one we meet."

—————————————

Who is the best friend of Hercules on *Hercules*?

Ultimate TV Trivia

Which *Hawaii Five-O* detective says, "Book 'em, Danno": Steve McGarrett, Ben Kokua or Chin Ho Kelly?

_ _ _ _ _ _ _ _

On *Lost in Space*, the Robinson family is bound for what section of the universe when their trip goes awry: Planet Kobal, Alpha Centauri Star System or Draconia?

_ _ _ _ _ _ _ _

Drew Carey and his friends work in a _____ _____on *The Drew Carey Show*.

_ _ _ _ _ _ _ _

What is the speedy name of the Hart's dog on *Hart to Hart*?

Ultimate TV Trivia

Which lady says, "Darling, I love you, but give me Park Avenue": Lisa Douglas (*Green Acres*), Miss Piggy (*The Muppet Show*) or Sue Ellen Ewing (*Dallas*)?

- - - - - - - -

In which state do high-society girls Paris Hilton and Nicole Richie experience farm life on the first season of *The Simple Life*?

- - - - - - - -

The toll-free hotline for *America's Most Wanted* is 1-800 _____.

- - - - - - - -

On *JAG*, which character was Colonel MacKenzie engaged to: Commander Rabb, Lt. Commander Brumby or Special Agent Webb?

Answers: ✂ Lisa Douglas ✂ Arkansas ✂ CRIME-TV ✂ Brumby

Ultimate TV Trivia™

Who says, "Nanu-Nanu": Commander Spock (*Star Trek*), Jeannie (*I Dream of Jeannie*) or Mork (*Mork and Mindy*)?

_ . _ . _ . _ . _ . _

In 2000, what network aired the shocking reality show *Who Wants to Marry a Millionaire*?

_ . _ . _ . _ . _ . _

Complete the name of this sci-fi television series: *Buck Rogers in the ____ Century.*

_ . _ . _ . _ . _ . _

Which relative lives with Carrie and Doug on *King of Queens*?

Answers: ✣ Mork ✣ FOX ✣ 25th ✣ Carrie's father

✣ 50 ✣

Ultimate TV Trivia™

Which *Three's Company* goofball said, "Eat your salad before it gets cold": Janet Dawson, Chrissy Snow or Stanley Roper?

— — — — — — — —

Where is Bernie Mac when he talks to his audience on *The Bernie Mac Show*?

— — — — — — — —

The producers of *Baywatch* launched a short-lived mystery spin-off of the series called _____ _____ in 1995.

— — — — — — — —

What is the name of the youngest Ingalls daughter? She was born during *Little House on the Prarie*'s fifth season.

Answers: ❖ Chrissy Snow ❖ Sitting in a chair ❖ *Baywatch Nights* ❖ Grace

Ultimate TV Trivia

 Who calls food "vittles": Granny Clampett (*Beverly Hillbillies*), Lucy Ricardo (*I Love Lucy*) or Barney Fife (*The Andy Griffith Show*)?

_ _ _ _ _ _ _ _

 In which state does *Dynasty*'s Blake Carrington find his black gold?

_ _ _ _ _ _ _ _

 Terminator heroine Linda Hamilton stars as a detective in love with a _____ in a 1980s mythical drama.

_ _ _ _ _ _ _ _

 The Wonder Years features three children in the Arnold family. Wayne and Kevin are the boys. Name their sister.

Ultimate TV Trivia

What talk show host caused uproar in the beef industry after saying, "It has just stopped me cold from eating another burger"?

In what east coast city does the drama *American Dreams* take place?

Jamie Sommers becomes the Bionic Woman after undergoing emergency surgery due to a _____ accident.

On the TV series *Kung Fu*, which relative is Kwai Chang Caine looking for?

Answers: ✿ Oprah Winfrey ✿ Philadelphia ✿ Parachuting
✿ His half-brother (Danny Caine)

Ultimate TV Trivia

 When asked if it was okay for cats to eat grass, which *Hollywood Squares* guest said, "Yes, It gives them a nice minty flavor": Animal (*The Muppet Show*), Alf (*ALF*) or Oscar the Grouch (*Sesame Street*)?

— .. — .. — .. — .. — ..

 What cable network shows the "Other Side" in *Crossing Over with John Edward*?

— .. — .. — .. — .. — ..

 Besides his lab coat, Bill Nye the Science Guy™ can be seen wearing a ____ ____ on each episode.

— .. — .. — .. — .. — ..

 What is the name of the only female rascal on *The Little Rascals*?

Answers: ✵ Alf ✵ Sci-Fi Channel ✵ Bow the ✵ Darla

Ultimate TV Trivia™

Who Said That?

On *Dragon Tales*, who says, "I wish, I wish with all my heart, to fly with dragons in a land apart": Zak and Wheezie, Cassie, or Emmy and Max?

Where Did It Happen?

On what news series can audiences find John Stossel, the "Give Me a Break" commentator: *60 Minutes*, *20/20* or *48 Hours*?

Blankety Blanks

Beavis and Butthead listen to _____ _____ music.

TV Life Real Life

On *Xena: Warrior Princess*, who is the royal one's loyal sidekick?

Answers: ❖ Emmy and Max ❖ *20/20* ❖ Heavy metal ❖ Gabrielle

Ultimate TV Trivia

On *Malcolm in the Middle*, who said, "You want to know the best part about childhood? At some point it stops": Reese, Malcolm or Dewey?

Where in Washington, D.C. does leading man Jack Mannion work on *The District*: the police department, the CIA or the Capitol building?

On the hour-long show _____ _____, detective Lily Rush investigates old unsolved crimes.

Barbara and Julie are Ann Romano's daughters on what '80s sitcom?

Answers: ❖ Malcolm ❖ The police department
Cold Case ❖ One Day at a Time

Ultimate TV Trivia

Who on *The Drew Carey Show* said, "Here's some advice: you're ugly": Mr. Wick, Drew or Mimi?

In what Colorado city does Dr. Mike of *Dr. Quinn, Medicine Woman* treat her patients?

Americans related to adolescent Kevin Arnold, played by _____ _____ in *The Wonder Years*.

What charming actress plays Kimberly, the oldest Brock sibling, on the TV drama *Picket Fences*?

Ultimate TV Trivia™

Who Said That?

What show uses the line, "I'm federal agent Jack Bauer and today is the longest day of my life"?

__ . __ . __ . __ . __

Where Did It Happen?

In what city does *The Apprentice* take place?

__ . __ . __ . __ . __

Blankety Blanks

Scooby Doo and his gang travel to their various adventures in a van called The _____ _____.

__ . __ . __ . __ . __

TV Life Real Life

Tenderheart, Love-a-lot and Funshine are all names of what group of cartoon characters?

Answers: ✧ 24 ✧ New York City ✧ Mystery Machine ✧ The Care Bears™

Ultimate TV Trivia

Who Said That?

Which *Beavis and Butthead* kid said, "Stop in the name of all that does not suck": Beavis, Butthead or Daria?

_ . _ . _ . _ . _

Where Did It Happen?

Where in Stuckyville does Ed Stevens of NBC's *Ed* run his law practice?

_ . _ . _ . _ . _

Blankety Blanks

On the classic detective series *Cagney and Lacey*, _____ is the tough one, while _____ shows her sensitive side.

_ . _ . _ . _ . _

TV Life Real Life

All in the Family's Archie Bunker calls his wife "Dingbat". What does he call his son-in-law?

Answers: ✧ Butthead ✧ In a bowling alley (Stucky Bowl) ✧ Cagney; Lacey ✧ Meathead

Ultimate TV Trivia™

A character on which TV classic said, "… we're already running an adoption agency, let's not start a matrimonial bureau": *The Patty Duke Show*, *The Donna Reed Show* or *The Doris Day Show*?

———————

Where can audiences find Paul Shaffer and his band each weekday evening?

———————

Caroline on *Caroline in the City* is the cartoonist drawing a comic strip similar to the actual comic strip _____.

———————

What is the name of Archie Andrews' best friend on *The Archie Show*?

Ultimate TV Trivia

A character on which medical drama said, "There's no crying in the OR. That's what the ladies room is for": *Chicago Hope*, *St. Elsewhere* or *ER*?

--- --- --- --- --- --- ---

In what city has chef Emeril Lagasse, star of *Emeril Live*, based his corporate headquarters?

--- --- --- --- --- --- ---

The series *Dark Angel* takes place in the year _____.

--- --- --- --- --- --- ---

What is the name of Speed Racer's girlfriend?

Answers: ❖ *ER* (Romano) ❖ New Orleans ❖ 2020 ❖ Trixie (*Speed Racer*)

Ultimate TV Trivia

The host of which game show says, "Survey says... ":
Family Feud, *Password* or *The Weakest Link*?

_ _ _ _ _ _ _ _

Short-lived medical dramas *MDs* and *Presidio Med* are
both based in what city's hospitals?

_ _ _ _ _ _ _ _

Since 1991, host Charlie _____ has interviewed thousands
of twentieth-century movers and shakers in his plain studio
with no live audience.

_ _ _ _ _ _ _ _

On *All My Children*, how are Stuart and Adam related?

Answers: ✷ *Family Feud* ✷ San Francisco ✷ Rose ✷ They are twin brothers.

Ultimate TV Trivia

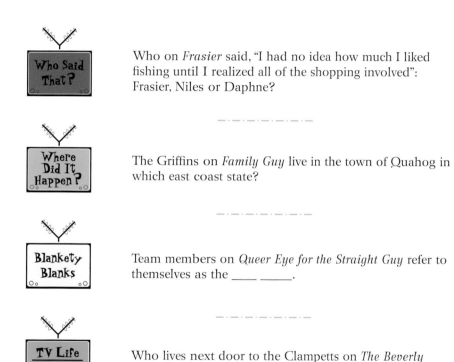

Who Said That?

Who on *Frasier* said, "I had no idea how much I liked fishing until I realized all of the shopping involved": Frasier, Niles or Daphne?

Where Did It Happen?

The Griffins on *Family Guy* live in the town of Quahog in which east coast state?

Blankety Blanks

Team members on *Queer Eye for the Straight Guy* refer to themselves as the ____ ____.

TV Life Real Life

Who lives next door to the Clampetts on *The Beverly Hillbillies*?

Answers: ❖ Niles ❖ Rhode Island ❖ Fab Five ❖ Mr. & Mrs. Drysdale

Ultimate TV Trivia™

What TV show starts with a voice-over narration that says, "He is immortal, born in the Highlands of Scotland 400 years ago"?

——————————————

Where do the fictitious characters Wembley, Gobo, Red and Mokey live?

——————————————

After a shocking first performance on *The Ed Sullivan Show*, singer _____ _____ was filmed above the waist for future appearances.

——————————————

On *One Life to Live*, who is Niki to Viki?

Answers: ❧ *The Highlander* ❧ *Fraggle Rock* ❧ Elvis Presley ❧ Niki is Viki's evil alter ego.

Ultimate TV Trivia

Who said, "Anyone who hates an octopus is warped": Gomez Addams (*The Addams Family*), Herman Munster (*The Munsters*) or Cliff Clavin (*Cheers*)?

Flipper was filmed off what state's shores?

Fill in the blanks for this *Fame* theme song: "I feel it coming together. People will ____ me and ____."

On *Jonny Quest*, how is Bandit related to Jonny?

Answers: ❖ Gomez Addams ❖ Florida ❖ See; cry ❖ He is Jonny's dog.

❖ 65 ❖

Ultimate TV Trivia™

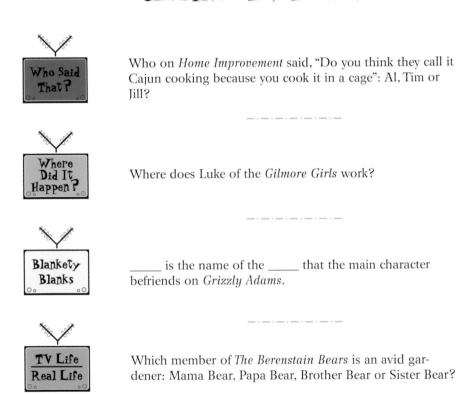

Who Said That?

Who on *Home Improvement* said, "Do you think they call it Cajun cooking because you cook it in a cage": Al, Tim or Jill?

Where Did It Happen?

Where does Luke of the *Gilmore Girls* work?

Blankety Blanks

_____ is the name of the _____ that the main character befriends on *Grizzly Adams*.

TV Life Real Life

Which member of *The Berenstain Bears* is an avid gardener: Mama Bear, Papa Bear, Brother Bear or Sister Bear?

Answers: ✷ Al ✷ At Luke's Coffee Shop ✷ Ben; bear ✷ Mama Bear

Ultimate TV Trivia™

Which *Howdy Doody* character says, "It's Howdy Doody time": Howdy Doody, Buffalo Bob or Clarabell the Clown?

_____

In what city, later to become the title of a soap spin-off, do the residents of *General Hospital* live?

_____

Gomer Pyle is an officer of the US _____ _____.

_____

On *Mister Rogers' Neighborhood*, what is the name of King Friday and Queen Sara's son?

Answers: ❖ Buffalo Bob ❖ Port Charles ❖ Marine Corps ❖ Prince Tuesday

Ultimate TV Trivia

Which cartoon character sings "My Darling Clementine": Yogi Bear, Snagglepuss or Huckleberry Hound?

_____

Where in New York does the Seaver family of *Growing Pains* live?

_____

_____ is the name of Gumby's claymation horse.

_____

How is Angelica Pickles related to Tommy Pickles in the cartoon series *Rugrats*™?

Ultimate TV Trivia™

On what show did Hades say, "Have your minions call my minions": *Hercules*, *Xena: Warrior Princess* or *He-Man*?

––– –– ––– –– ––– –– –––

Where do the characters on the British comedy *Fawlty Towers* work?

––– –– ––– –– ––– –– –––

Foghorn _____ is the name of the brassy rooster on *Looney Tunes*™.

––– –– ––– –– ––– –– –––

On *High Chaparral*, how are Buck and Billy Blue related?

Answers: ❖ *Hercules* ❖ In a hotel (Fawlty Towers Hotel) Leghorn ❖ Buck is Billy Blue's uncle.

❖ 69 ❖

Ultimate TV Trivia

Which TV hero said, "… you wouldn't like me when I'm angry"?

_._._._._._._

Where do the *Head of the Class* students attend school: Clayton High School, Monroe High School or Washington High School?

_._._._._._._

Mark Cooper of *Hangin' with Mr. Cooper* is a former _____ player.

_._._._._._._

Name the detective series where Buddy Ebsen and Lee Meriwether team up as father and daughter.

Ultimate TV Trivia

The star of what sitcom often starts a sentence with the phrase, "You might be a redneck if ...": *Grace Under Fire*, *Roseanne* or *The Jeff Foxworthy Show*?

_ . _ . _ . _ . _ . _

Where were the first five seasons of *The X-Files* shot?

_ . _ . _ . _ . _ . _

Angel Jonathan Smith of *Highway to Heaven* refers to God as the _____, instead of using his formal title.

_ . _ . _ . _ . _ . _

How is the victim on *The Fugitive* related to the title character?

Answers: ✷ *The Jeff Foxworthy Show* ✷ Vancouver, British Columbia Boss ✷ She is his wife.

Ultimate TV Trivia

What comedy show had a regular sketch where the audience heard the phrase "I am crushing your head": *Saturday Night Live, In Living Color* or *Kids in the Hall*?

What is Sergeant Carter's hopping hometown on *Hogan's Heroes*?

The original _____ ____ _____ show premiered in 1976. This brother and sister team became the youngest co-hosts of a weekly TV variety show.

What 1980s TV show features two brothers named Rick and A.J.?

Ultimate TV Trivia

Who Said That?

Who said, "What's Wal-Mart™? Do they sell walls there": Paris Hilton, Sharon Osbourne or Donald Trump?

_ _ _ _ _ _ _ _

Where Did It Happen?

On *The Honeymooners*, where does Ralph Kramden work in Brooklyn?

_ _ _ _ _ _ _ _

Blankety Blanks

After every *The Price is Right* show, Bob Barker reminds audiences to _____ or _____ their pets.

_ _ _ _ _ _ _ _

TV Life Real Life

On *Charlie's Angels*, who plays Kris, the sister of Jill Munroe?

Answers: ✧ Paris Hilton ✧ Gotham Bus Company ✧ Spay; neuter ✧ Cheryl Ladd

Ultimate TV Trivia

What late-night talk show host said, "Okay, Max. You play one of those songs that you play while I go over here and adjust my underwear": David Letterman, Conan O'Brien or Jimmy Kimmel?

In what city does the drama *Rescue Me* take place?

Audiences never see all of neighbor Wilson's _____ on *Home Improvement*.

What is the name of Tony Baretta's pet cockatoo on the '70s police drama *Baretta*?

Ultimate TV Trivia

On what show is the following quote heard before each episode, "There is a fifth dimension beyond that which is known to man"?

Hotel's fictitious St. Gregory Hotel was patterned after a hotel in which San Francisco district: Union Square, Nob Hill or North Beach?

The group of kids on *The Howdy Doody Show* is known as The _____ Gallery.

How was talk show master Phil Donahue related to the late actor/producer Danny Thomas?

Answers: ❖ *The Twilight Zone* ❖ Nob Hill (The Fairmont) Peanut ❖ Phil was Danny Thomas' son-in-law. (Phil is married to actress Marlo Thomas.)

Ultimate TV Trivia

Who Said That?

Which *Roseanne* kid asked, "Do we have to go in the Big and Fat store": Becky, Darlene or D.J.?

_ _ _ _ _ _ _

Where Did It Happen?

At which US landmark do Bobby and Cindy get lost during one of the Brady Bunch family vacations?

_ _ _ _ _ _ _

Blankety Blanks

The contestants on *Iron Chef* have one _____ to prepare a _____ using a featured ingredient.

_ _ _ _ _ _ _

TV Life / Real Life

News correspondent Maria Shriver is the niece of what former US president?

Answers: ❖ D.J. ❖ The Grand Canyon ❖ Hour: meal ❖ John F. Kennedy

Ultimate TV Trivia™

What show uses the tagline "The Power of Three Will Set You Free"?

Where does Jamie on *The Jamie Foxx Show* work: Kings Tower Hotel, Queens Tower Hotel or The Princess Suites?

In the '80s cartoon series *Jem*, the main character plays in a band called the _____.

Sharon Osbourne and rocker Ozzy of *The Osbournes* have how many children together?

Answers: ❖ *Charmed* ❖ Kings Tower Hotel ❖ Holograms ❖ Three (Aimee, Kelly and Jack)

Ultimate TV Trivia™

What show uses the tagline "Spying. Stealing. Murder. And You Think Your Family Has Issues": *The Sopranos*, *Dynasty* or *Alias*?

—— —— —— —— ——

Joan Girardi is a modern-day Joan of Arc in what city?

—— —— —— —— ——

Alexandra's cat, _____, is the band mascot on *Josie and the Pussycats*.

—— —— —— —— ——

What famous comedian and star of the *Texaco Star Theater* was a mainstay on TV for decades, earning him the nickname "Mr. Television?"

Answers: ❖ *Alias* ❖ Arcadia (*Joan of Arcadia*) ❖ Sebastian ❖ Milton Berle

Ultimate TV Trivia

Who Said That?

What cartoon pair sings, "Happy, happy, joy, joy"?

Where Did It Happen?

In what state do the aliens on *3rd Rock From the Sun* land when they arrive on Earth?

Blankety Blanks

Court TV touts itself as The _____ Channel.

TV Life Real Life

What is the relationship between Comedy Central's Joe Rogan and Doug Stanhope?

Answers: ❖ Ren & Stimpy ❖ Ohio ❖ Investigation ❖ They are both hosts of *The Man Show*.

Ultimate TV Trivia™

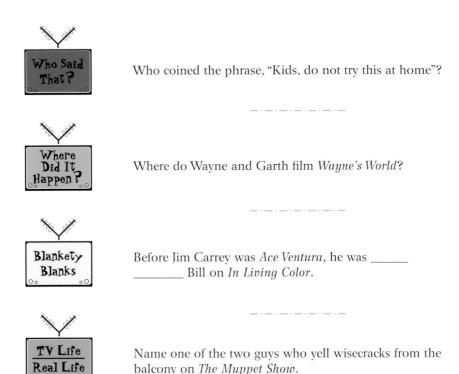

Who Said That?

Who coined the phrase, "Kids, do not try this at home"?

—·—·—·—·—·—·—·—

Where Did It Happen?

Where do Wayne and Garth film *Wayne's World*?

—·—·—·—·—·—·—·—

Blankety Blanks

Before Jim Carrey was *Ace Ventura*, he was _____ _____ Bill on *In Living Color*.

—·—·—·—·—·—·—·—

TV Life Real Life

Name one of the two guys who yell wisecracks from the balcony on *The Muppet Show*.

Answers: ❧ Evel Knievel (ABC's *Wide World of Sports*) ❧ In the basement of Wayne's house ❧ Fire Marshall ❧ Waldorf; Statler

❧ 80 ❧

Ultimate TV Trivia™

Who Said That?

What *Looney Tunes*™ character says, "Oh, you have made me very angry, very angry indeed": Marvin the Martian, Elmer Fudd or Sylvester the Cat?

Where Did It Happen?

What cartoon TV family lives in Heimlich County, Texas?

Blankety Blanks

The initials __ __ __ stand for the delivery company Doug works for on *King of Queens*.

TV Life Real Life

How many siblings is Charlie Salinger left to care for on *Party of Five*?

Ultimate TV Trivia

 On what sitcom is the greeting, "Hello, Newman," heard when Wayne Knight's character walks into a room?

_____

 In what community do neighbors Gary Ewing, Karen Fairgate, Kenny Ward and Laura Avery live?

_____

 The name of the shipwrecked boat on *Gilligan's Island* is the __ __ _____.

_____

 Which *ER* doctor has a hearing-impaired son named Reese?

Answers: ✿ *Seinfeld* ✿ Knots Landing ✿ *S.S. Minnow* ✿ Dr. Peter Benton

✿ 82 ✿

Ultimate TV Trivia

Which fashionable TV character said, "Oh, my god; She's fashion road kill"?

_____

What is the name of the resort and casino where the characters of NBC's *Las Vegas* mingle?

_____

High school teacher Ralph Hinkley dons a _____-colored suit that gives him superhuman powers on *The Greatest American Hero*.

_____

Which member of the Brock family is a doctor on *Picket Fences*?

Answers: ✧ Samantha Jones (*Sex and the City*) ✧ Montecito ✧ Red ✧ The mother (Jill)

Ultimate TV Trivia™

Which talk show host ends each segment by saying, "Take care of yourself and each other": Maury Povich, Jerry Springer or Montel Williams?

_ . _ . _ . _ . _ . _

What '70s musical television family lives at 698 Sycamore Road, San Pueblo, CA?

_ . _ . _ . _ . _ . _

Maddie and David, played by Cybill Shepherd and Bruce Willis, work at the _____ _____ Detective Agency on *Moonlighting*.

_ . _ . _ . _ . _ . _

On *Providence*, which of Sydney's deceased family members imparts advice to Sydney in her dreams?

Ultimate TV Trivia

What TV good guy said, "Why? Got some?" in response to the question, "I suppose you can make an explosive out of chewing gum"?

-- -- -- -- -- -- --

Do *thirtysomething's* Michael and Hope Steadman live in Philadelphia, Boston or Providence?

-- -- -- -- -- -- --

Miami Vice's Sonny Crockett lives on a sailboat guarded by his pet _____, Elvis.

-- -- -- -- -- -- --

What family does ALF live with after his spaceship crashes into their garage?

Answers: ✣ (Angus) MacGyver ✣ Philadelphia ✣ Alligator ✣ The Tanners

Ultimate TV Trivia™

Which late night talk show host said, "Everyone has a purpose in life. Perhaps yours is watching television": Johnny Carson, David Letterman or Jimmy Kimmel?

Tony Micelli and his daughter Samantha on *Who's The Boss?* moved from Brooklyn to live and work with a family in which state?

Realizing he is the only member of *The Brady Bunch* without a trophy, Bobby enters a/an ___ _____ eating contest.

What long-running sitcom stars Cory and Topanga as high-school sweethearts who end up marrying?

Answers: ❖ David Letterman ❖ Connecticut ❖ Ice cream ❖ *Boy Meets World*

Ultimate TV Trivia™

Which TV wife said to her husband, "Quick, they're gone. Change the locks." when their kids left for school: Roseanne (*Roseanne*), Debra (*Everybody Loves Raymond*) or Peggy Bundy (*Married. . . with Children*)?

To which floor does Claudia of *Less Than Perfect* move after receiving a promotion?

Kim Parker, the younger half of the mother-daughter comedy *The Parkers*, was originally a character on the UPN comedy _____.

Who is the "ugly" family member on *The Munsters*?

Answers: ✧ *Roseanne* ✧ The 22nd ✧ *Moesha* ✧ Marilyn

Ultimate TV Trivia

Which cartoon character said, "I'm not fat, I'm big boned": Homer (*The Simpsons*), Cartman (*South Park*) or Patrick (*SpongeBob™ SquarePants*)?

--- --- --- --- ---

What comedy takes place in Sacred Heart Hospital?

--- --- --- --- ---

Just the Ten of Us, featuring Coach Lubbock and his family, is a spin-off of the popular family sitcom _____ _____.

--- --- --- --- ---

Whose "animated" birth was featured on one of the most popular TV episodes of the 1960s?

Answers: ❖ Cartman ❖ *Scrubs* ❖ *Growing Pains* ❖ Pebbles Flintstone (*The Flintstones*)

Ultimate TV Trivia™

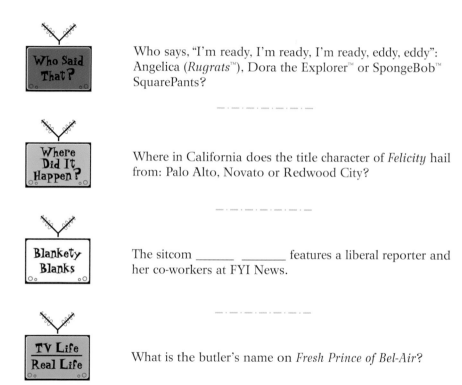

Who Said That?

Who says, "I'm ready, I'm ready, I'm ready, eddy, eddy": Angelica (*Rugrats*™), Dora the Explorer™ or SpongeBob™ SquarePants?

Where Did It Happen?

Where in California does the title character of *Felicity* hail from: Palo Alto, Novato or Redwood City?

Blankety Blanks

The sitcom _____ _____ features a liberal reporter and her co-workers at FYI News.

TV Life / Real Life

What is the butler's name on *Fresh Prince of Bel-Air*?

Ultimate TV Trivia

Who Said That?

Who often shouts, "Bam!" on his cooking show?

_____

Where Did It Happen?

What is the name of the maximum-security prison that is the setting for HBO's *Oz*?

_____

Blankety Blanks

During the final season of _____, the family wins $108 million in the Illinois lotto.

_____

TV Life Real Life

Before becoming Eastland's beloved housemother on *The Facts of Life*, Edna Garrett was the family maid on what show?

Ultimate TV Trivia™

Which character on *The Waltons* said, "I could do with another sandwich, Esther": John, Jim-Bob or Grandpa?

Where does Joey from *Friends* move to in his spin-off series, *Joey*?

Pete the Pup on *The Little Rascals* has a circle around his _____ eye.

On the short-lived but well-loved series *Freaks and Geeks*, is Lindsay Weir a freak or a geek?

Ultimate TV Trivia™

Which animated character says, "Whoa, Momma": Johnny Bravo, Daffy Duck or Little Bill?

_._._.._.._._

Where did *Mad About You* characters Paul and Jamie first meet: at a newsstand, a diner or a movie theater?

_._._.._.._._

The time- and body-jumping adventures of Dr. Sam Beckett are chronicled in the show _____ ____.

_._._.._.._._

On *Little House on the Prairie*, what is the nickname of Laura Ingalls-Wilder's husband?

Answers: ✵ Johnny Bravo ✵ A newsstand ✵ *Quantum Leap*
✵ Manley (short for Almanzo)

Ultimate TV Trivia™

On what '80s comedy does Larry say, "I'm Larry. This is my brother Darryl and this is my other brother Darryl"?

_ _ _ _ _ _ _ _ _

Chicago's Cook County General is the workplace of characters on what hospital drama?

_ _ _ _ _ _ _ _ _

Talk show host _____ _____ gave Tickle Me Elmo a boost when the doll was distributed to audience members.

_ _ _ _ _ _ _ _ _

On *The Dukes of Hazzard*, how are Bo and Luke Duke related?

Answers: ❖ *Newhart* ❖ *ER* ❖ Rosie O'Donnell ❖ They are cousins.

Ultimate TV Trivia™

What animated super hero says, "Up and at 'em," followed by his name?

— — — — — — — —

What is the name of the small New York company where the sitcom *Taxi* takes place?

— — — — — — — —

The character Audrey on TV's *Ellen* always wears the color _____.

— — — — — — — —

Who is the English teacher on *Fame*?

Ultimate TV Trivia™

Who says, "God'll get you for that": Maude (*Maude*), Lucy (*I Love Lucy*) or Sophia (*The Golden Girls*)?

_ _ _ _ _ _ _ _ _ _

Where does Snoopy find his previous owner on *Snoopy, Come Home*?

_ _ _ _ _ _ _ _ _ _

Sci-fi TV cult favorite _____ _____ _____ ____, also known as *MST3K*, features movie commentary from both humans and robots.

_ _ _ _ _ _ _ _ _ _

On November 22, 1953, what hilarious variety show went on the air live as the very first color TV broadcast in history: *The Milton Berle Show*, *The Colgate Comedy Hour* or *Bonanza*?

Answers: ❖ Maude ❖ A hospital ❖ *Mystery Science Theater 3000* ❖ *The Colgate Comedy Hour*

Ultimate TV Trivia™

On the cartoon *SpongeBob™ SquarePants*, who says, "Meow, meow, meow": Gary, Mr. Krabs or Patrick?

—— —— —— —— ——

What cartoon father works at Spacely's Sprockets?

—— —— —— —— ——

Family Ties character Alex Keaton, played by Michael J. Fox, idolizes public figure _____ _____.

—— —— —— —— ——

Henry Mancini was nominated for an Emmy and won two Grammys for an album of music from what '50s crime drama about a stylishly cool private eye?

Answers: ❖ Gary (SpongeBob™'s pet snail) ❖ George Jetson ❖ Richard Nixon ❖ *Peter Gunn*

Ultimate TV Trivia

On what show do audiences hear the quote: "And now for something completely different": *Saturday Night Live*, *Monty Python's Flying Circus* or *In Living Color*?

_ . _ . _ . _ . _ . _

Wile E. Coyote uses what company's products to try and catch the Road Runner?

_ . _ . _ . _ . _ . _

Host Chuck Woolery helped hook up couples looking for romance on _____ _____ in the 1980s.

_ . _ . _ . _ . _ . _

Name the first British TV program sold to a US network about a British spy named Steed and his female partners.

Answers: ❖ *Monty Python's Flying Circus* ❖ The ACME Corporation ❖ *Love Connection* ❖ *The Avengers*

Ultimate TV Trivia

Which news correspondent said, "I'd rather work with someone who's good at their job but doesn't like me, than someone who likes me but is a ninny": Dan Rather, Tom Brokaw or Sam Donaldson?

In what city do most of the events on *All My Children* take place?

The Fall Guy features bounty hunters who also work in the movies as _____.

On *The Anna Nicole Show*, who is Sugar Pie?

Answers: ❖ Sam Donaldson ❖ Pine Valley ❖ Stuntmen ❖ Anna's dog

Ultimate TV Trivia

Who Said That?

Who said, "Mmmmm . . . forbidden donut"?

––––––––––––––––

Where Did It Happen?

Which soap takes place in the fictional town of Oakdale: *Days of our Lives*, *As the The World Turns* or *Guiding Light*?

––––––––––––––––

Blankety Blanks

Cheers bar manager Sam "Mayday" Malone used to pitch for the _____ ___ ___ baseball team.

––––––––––––––––

TV Life Real Life

On *Leave it to Beaver*, what is the Beaver's real first name?

Answers: ❖ Homer Simpson ❖ *As the World Turns*
❖ Boston Red Sox ❖ Theodore

❖ 99 ❖

66

Ultimate TV Trivia

 The quote, "O'Reilly, I have seen more intelligent creatures than you lying on their backs at the bottoms of ponds," was heard on which British comedy: *Mr. Bean*, *Fawlty Towers* or *Keeping Up Appearances*?

 One Life to Live takes place in the fictional town of Llanview in which state: Massachusetts, Pennsylvania or Connecticut?

 The *Falcon Crest* family owns a _____ that produces their fortune.

 What do the initials B.J. stand for on *B.J. and the Bear*?

Answers: ✣ *Fawlty Towers* ✣ Pennsylvania ✣ Winery ✣ Billie Joe

Ultimate TV Trivia

 Which commentator said, "Don't rule out working with your hands. It does not preclude using your head": David Brinkley, Andy Rooney or Maria Shriver?

--- · --- · ---

 On *The Bold and the Beautiful*, the Forrester family rules from their luxurious mansion in which city: Beverly Hills, Miami Beach or Palm Springs?

--- · --- · ---

 Crossover character _____ _____ bridged the gap from *Beverly Hills, 90210* to *Melrose Place*.

--- · --- · ---

 What is strange about Jamie's sister, Vicki, on *Small Wonder*?

Answers: ✵ Andy Rooney ✵ Beverly Hills ✵ Jake Hanson ✵ Vicki is a robot.

Ultimate TV Trivia™

Which host said, "Democracy means that anyone can grow up to be president, and anyone who doesn't grow up can be vice president": Bill Maher, Jon Stewart or Johnny Carson?

_ _ _ _ _ _ _ _

Which soap opera takes place in the fictional town of Bay City: *Another World*, *Days of Our Lives* or *Falcon Crest*?

_ _ _ _ _ _ _ _

The color of Pee Wee Herman's signature _____ is red.

_ _ _ _ _ _ _ _

What famous rock drummer inspired Animal, a drum-beating character on *The Muppet Show*?

Answers: ❖ Johnny Carson ❖ *Another World* ❖ Bowtie ❖ Keith Moon of The Who

Ultimate TV Trivia

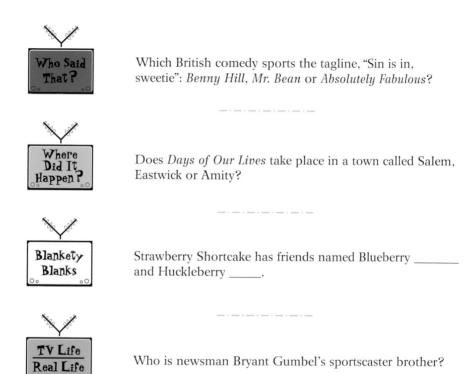

Who Said That?

Which British comedy sports the tagline, "Sin is in, sweetie": *Benny Hill*, *Mr. Bean* or *Absolutely Fabulous*?

Where Did It Happen?

Does *Days of Our Lives* take place in a town called Salem, Eastwick or Amity?

Blankety Blanks

Strawberry Shortcake has friends named Blueberry _____ and Huckleberry _____.

TV Life Real Life

Who is newsman Bryant Gumbel's sportscaster brother?

Answers: ❖ *Absolutely Fabulous* ❖ Salem ❖ Muffin; Pie ❖ Greg Gumbel

Ultimate TV Trivia

Which TV host often calls her co-host "Big Daddy": Katie Couric, Kelly Ripa or Jane Pauley?

___ ___ ___ ___ ___

Where does the Berenstain Bear family make its home?

___ ___ ___ ___ ___

TV detective _____ is known for sucking on a _____.

___ ___ ___ ___ ___

What *Match Game* regular, who sparred with Charles Nelson Reilly, was first booked on the show only because her husband, Jack Klugman, said he wouldn't appear without her?

Ultimate TV Trivia™

What PBS character sings, "I love you. You love me. We're a happy family ..."?

––––––––––

On *The Powerpuff Girls*, three super-powered little girls try to save what city from monsters?

––––––––––

The kids show *The Electric Company* regularly aired *The _____ of _____*, featuring short clips of the superhero in action.

––––––––––

Name the characters who make up the *Odd Couple*.

Ultimate TV Trivia

Which *Xena: Warrior Princess* character said, "Choose the one drink you wouldn't give your worst enemy, and give me a double": Joxer, Autolycus or Callisto?

—————————————

On his show, Mister Rogers visits King Friday, Henrietta Pussycat, X the Owl and other characters who all live where?

—————————————

On the television show *Wonder Woman*, _____ Prince changes into Wonder Woman by _____ _____.

—————————————

What are the first names (also the girls' real names) of the sisters on *Sister, Sister*?

Ultimate TV Trivia™

Who on *The West Wing* said, "By the way, my Princeton Tigers could whip your Cal Bears any day of the week": Toby, C.J. or Sam?

Where do the Teletubbies™ live?

_____ _____ _____ debuted in 1970 with Howard Cosell, Keith Jackson and Don Meredith giving pithy play-by-play and colorful commentary.

Which comedian appeared on *The Mike Douglas Show* playing violin with his sister: Jerry Seinfeld, Ben Stiller or Adam Sandler?

Answers: ❖ Sam ❖ Teletubbyland ❖ *Monday Night Football* ❖ Ben Stiller

Ultimate TV Trivia™

On what show is the following quote heard, "Growing up happens in a heartbeat. One day you're in diapers; the next day you're gone": *Growing Pains*, *The Wonder Years* or *My So-Called Life*?

Where does SpongeBob™ SquarePants work?

In 1979, mischievous magpies _____ and _____ shared billing with Mighty Mouse in an animated TV series.

Is Boom Boom, Harley or Froggy the nickname of *Welcome Back, Kotter*'s Freddie Washington?

Ultimate TV Trivia

On what show does the host ask contestants, "Is that your final answer?"

On the cartoon *Dexter's Laboratory*, Dexter's secret lab is hidden in which room of his house?

On *I Spy*, Bill Cosby and Robert Culp are undercover secret agents posing as a _____ player and his trainer.

Which woman on *Sex and the City* converts to Judaism in order to appease her boyfriend's family: Miranda, Charlotte or Carrie?

Answers: ✣ *Who Wants to Be a Millionaire?* ✣ His bedroom ✣ Tennis ✣ Charlotte

Ultimate TV Trivia

The host of which game show says, "You leave with nothing," to a losing contestant: *Wheel of Fortune*, *Pyramid* or *The Weakest Link*?

—·—·—·—·—·—

On the cartoon *Magilla Gorilla*, where does Mr. Peebles work everyday?

—·—·—·—·—·—

Featuring Goldie Hawn and Lily Tomlin, _____ had shtick that stuck, enjoying a six-season run.

—·—·—·—·—·—

Which TV couple was married on their first date: Dharma and Greg (*Dharma and Greg*), Heathcliff and Clair (*The Cosby Show*) or Peggy and Al (*Married... With Children*)?

Answers: ❖ *The Weakest Link* ❖ In his pet shop ❖ *Laugh-In* ❖ Dharma and Greg

Ultimate TV Trivia

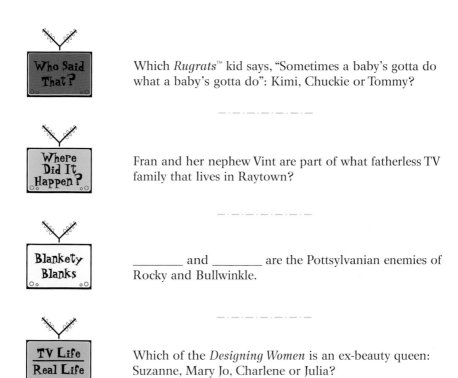

Who Said That?

Which *Rugrats*™ kid says, "Sometimes a baby's gotta do what a baby's gotta do": Kimi, Chuckie or Tommy?

Where Did It Happen?

Fran and her nephew Vint are part of what fatherless TV family that lives in Raytown?

Blankety Blanks

_____ and _____ are the Pottsylvanian enemies of Rocky and Bullwinkle.

TV Life Real Life

Which of the *Designing Women* is an ex-beauty queen: Suzanne, Mary Jo, Charlene or Julia?

Ultimate TV Trivia

Who said, "You're a public defender. You stand for the underprivileged. I'm a bailiff. I stand. Kind of like cattle": a character on *Night Court*, *Judge Judy* or *Ally McBeal*?

Does Quick Draw McGraw work as a US marshall in Arizona, New Mexico or Oklahoma?

Star Trek's Mr. Spock is half _____ and half _____.

What is the name of the elderly man who adopts Punky Brewster and her dog Brandon?

Answers: ✥ *Night Court* (Bull) ✥ New Mexico ✥ Human; Vulcan ✥ Henry (Warnimont)

Ultimate TV Trivia

What Nickelodeon™ cartoon character says, "Vamanos"?

-·-·-·-·-·-

Where do the Smurfs live?

-·-·-·-·-·-

Red Skelton plays Clem_____, Freddie the
_____ and the Mean Widdle Kid on the *The Red Skelton Show*.

-·-·-·-·-·-

What last name do Ozzie and Harriet share on *The Adventures of Ozzie and Harriet*?

Ultimate TV Trivia

Who on *Murphy Brown* said, "I'd like to think that one day people won't be judged by their color or their gender, but by the thing that really matters – their taste in music": Corky, Jim or Murphy?

Which of the following shows did *not* take place in New York: *Kojak*, *McCloud* or *Barnaby Jones*?

Goofy, _____, _____ and _____ make up Disney™'s *Goof Troop*.

On *The Smothers Brothers Comedy Hour*, which brother plays bass: Tommy or Dick?

Answers: ✧ Murphy ✧ Barnaby Jones ✧ Pete, Max and PJ ✧ Dick (Tommy plays guitar.)

Ultimate TV Trivia™

Who on *The Mary Tyler Moore Show* said, "Tell me Mary, do you think a single raw carrot would put any more ugly fat on me": Sue Ann, Lou or Murray?

In what west coast city is Stewart McMillan the police commissioner on *McMillan and Wife*?

On the *Looney Tunes*™ episode "Hare Tonic," _____ _____ convinces Elmer Fudd that he has a disease called Rabbititus.

Despite its title, on what '50s show is Margaret Anderson sometimes right and her husband, Jim, wrong?

Ultimate TV Trivia™

A character from which show said, "I know who Gauguin is; he paints naked girls": *Moonlighting*, *Matlock* or *Nash Bridges*?

—————————

Does *Perry Mason* take place in Los Angeles, Chicago or New York?

—————————

The absentee author and landlord in the detective show _____ ____ is Robin Masters.

—————————

What famous country star provides the voice of the Balladeer for every episode of *The Dukes of Hazzard*, as well as singing its theme song?

Ultimate TV Trivia

 Which cartoon character says, "Here I come to save the day"?

_____

 On *The Man from U.N.C.L.E.*, is the secret entrance to headquarters through a barbershop, dry cleaners or shoeshine shop?

_____

 By the end of 2003, soap opera character Erica Kane of *All My Children* had been married ____ times.

_____

 The *Mod Squad*'s original trio includes Pete, Julie and which other character?

Answers: ❖ Mighty Mouse ❖ A dry cleaners ❖ Nine (to six different men) ❖ Linc

Ultimate TV Trivia™

Who said, "Boy, I'm never going to high school if they make you call girls": Beaver Cleaver, Bobby Brady or Chip Douglas?

_._._._._._

Is Dodge City, Kansas, the primary location of *Gunsmoke*, *Bonanza* or *The Virginian*?

_._._._._._

Fill in this soap opera introduction: "Like _____ through the _____ . . . so are the *Days of Our Lives*.

_._._._._._

Name the two Hackett brothers who run a private airline on *Wings*.

Ultimate TV Trivia

Who on *Friends* said, "All right. You're a monkey. You're loose in the city. Where do you go": Joey, Chandler or Ross?

Describe the house where Jim Rockford of *The Rockford Files* lives.

On the soap opera *Passions*, the character Tabitha Lenox is known for being a _____.

Name *The Carol Burnett Show* comedienne whose resemblance to the show's main star helped get her the part.

Answers: ✦ Ross ✦ It is a trailer. ✦ Witch ✦ Vicki Lawrence

Ultimate TV Trivia

Which correspondent said, "An intellectual snob is someone who can listen to the 'William Tell Overture' and not think of the Lone Ranger": Dan Rather, Andy Rooney or Stone Philips?

Where in the south does *Bonanza*'s Ben Cartwright go to meet Little Joe's mother?

On *General Hospital*, actor Anthony Geary plays the role of both _____ and _____ at the same time.

What does Polly, wife of Major John D. MacGillis, do for a living on *Major Dad*?

Answers: ❖ Dan Rather ❖ New Orleans ❖ Luke; Bill (Luke's cousin) ❖ She is a reporter.

Ultimate TV Trivia

Who said, "If you were singing like this two thousand years ago, people would have stoned you"?

_._._._._._._._

Where do characters on *Bonanza* go to find fresh water by heading north from the Ponderosa?

_._._._._._._._

_____ _____ sings the theme song "Love and Marriage" for the show *Married . . . with Children*?

_._._._._._._._

What type of work does Eldin on *Murphy Brown* do for Murphy?

Ultimate TV Trivia

 On what PBS series might you hear the words, "as is," "bisque," "inlay," "glaze" and "original finish"?

_ . _ . _ . _ . _ . _ . _

 The Phoenix Foundation employs which of the following characters: MacGyver, Lovejoy or Spenser?

_ . _ . _ . _ . _ . _ . _

 The daytime soap *Another World* was conceived as a spin-off of the soap ___ ___ ___ ___.

_ . _ . _ . _ . _ . _ . _

 Comedic actor Benny Hill's (*The Benny Hill Show*) real name was Alfred Hawthorn Hill; however, he adopted the stage name Benny in homage to what great comedian?

Answers: ❖ *Antiques Roadshow* ❖ MacGyver (*MacGyver*) ❖ *As the World Turns* ❖ Jack Benny

Ultimate TV Trivia

What late night host said, "Here's something to think about: How come you never see a headline like 'Psychic Wins Lottery'": Jimmy Kimmel, Jay Leno or Craig Kilborn?

In what western city does Robert Uhrich work in his first detective series as Dan Tanna?

If you hear people speaking "Ubbi Dubbi," you are watching the kids' PBS TV show _____.

Which of Fox Mulder's relatives on the *The X-Files* is kidnapped and never found?

Answers: ❖ Jay Leno ❖ Las Vegas (*Vegas*) ❖ *Zoom* ❖ His sister.

Ultimate TV Trivia™

 Who Said That?
On what show is the sentence, "Homey don't play dat," heard?

_ _ _ _ _ _ _ _ _ _ _

 Where Did It Happen?
What Chicago-based TV show features characters like Frank Nitty, Al Capone and Eliot Ness?

_ _ _ _ _ _ _ _ _ _ _

 Blankety Blanks
On the PBS kids series _Between the Lions_, Martha Reader and the _____ entertain with a repertoire consisting of only vowel sounds.

_ _ _ _ _ _ _ _ _ _ _

 TV Life Real Life
What is Dennis' last name on _Dennis the Menace_?

Answers: ☆ _In Living Color_ ☆ _The Untouchables_ ☆ Vowelles ☆ Mitchell

Ultimate TV Trivia™

Who on *Ally McBeal* said, "I can't do anything about it, but I'd be happy to sympathize": Ally, Renee or Richard?

_ _ _ _ _ _ _ _ _ _

The Oprah Winfrey show is based in what US city?

_ _ _ _ _ _ _ _ _ _

The cartoon *Jabberjaw* stars a great white shark who plays the _____ in the band called The Neptunes.

_ _ _ _ _ _ _ _ _ _

Cybill's two ex-husbands on *Cybill* are Ira and Jeff. Is Jeff the stuntman or the novelist?

Answers: ☆ Richard ☆ Chicago ☆ Drums ☆ The stuntman

Ultimate TV Trivia™

Sergeant Phil Esterhaus ends each roll call with, "…let's be careful out there," on what police drama?

— — — — — — — —

On *The Sharon Osbourne* show, from where on stage does Sharon often interview her guest?

— — — — — — — —

The PBS series _____ stars a friendly canine with an overactive imagination.

— — — — — — — —

What TV star was the first (and only) woman summoned by Johnny Carson to sit down with him after her stand-up comedy act?

Answers: ✵ *Hill Street Blues* ✵ A bed ✵ *Wishbone* ✵ Ellen DeGeneres

Ultimate TV Trivia

Who says, "Here come da judge": Bill Cosby (*The Cosby Show*), Flip Wilson (*The Flip Wilson Show*) or Red Skelton (*The Red Skelton Show*)?

The *Late Show with David Letterman* is taped in the theatre formerly used for what famous television icon's broadcasts?

Roots star and Emmy-winning actor LeVar Burton hosts the educational children's program _____ _____.

Roxie Roker, who played Helen Willis on *The Jeffersons*, is the mother of what famous musician?

Ultimate TV Trivia™

Who on *I Love Lucy* said, "Oh, Lucy – you're not getting another idea, are you": Ethel Mertz, Desi Arnaz or Fred Mertz?

- - - - - - -

Is *The Tonight Show with Jay Leno* taped in California's downtown Hollywood, Burbank or Studio City?

- - - - - - -

The four Teletubbies™ are named Po, Laa-Laa, _____ and _____ _____.

- - - - - - -

Name the folk musician father of Mackenzie Phillips, star of *One Day at a Time*.

Answers: ✦ Ethel Mertz ✦ Burbank ✦ Dipsy; Tinky Winky ✦ John Phillips (of The Mamas and the Papas)

Ultimate TV Trivia

Who says, "Oh, my stars": Samantha Stephens (*Bewitched*), Eddie Haskell (*Leave it to Beaver*) or Trixie Norton (*The Honeymooners*)?

Where did talk show host Jenny Jones win big before getting her own talk show: *The Price is Right*, *Press Your Luck* or *Jeopardy*?

Seen in more than 100 countries, _____ is the most watched science television series in the world and the most watched documentary series on PBS.

In which film did *Blossom*'s Mayim Bialik portray Bette Midler's character as a young girl?

Answers: ❖ Samantha Stephens ❖ *Press Your Luck* (She also played on *Match Game*.) ❖ *Nova* ❖ *Beaches*

Ultimate TV Trivia

During a televised mission, which astronaut said, "Houston, Tranquility Base here. The Eagle has landed"?

_ _ _ _ _ _ _ _ _

In which US state did late night masters Jay Leno and Conan O'Brien grow up?

_ _ _ _ _ _ _ _ _

Actor _____ _____ hosts the PBS science series *Scientific Frontiers*.

_ _ _ _ _ _ _ _ _

Lizzie McGuire's Hilary Duff is an accomplished performer of what type of dance?

Ultimate TV Trivia

Who says, "You big dummy": Lamont Sanford (*Sanford & Son*), Fred Sanford (*Sanford & Son*) or Moms Mabely (*The Merv Griffin Show*)?

On which late-night show did Triumph, the insult comic dog, get his big break?

On the animated series *The Powerpuff Girls*, the three super-powered little girls are named Blossom, Bubbles and

_____.

Name an original cast member of *The Facts of Life* who appeared in the movie *The Breakfast Club*.

Answers: ✧ Fred Sanford ✧ *Late Night with Conan O'Brien* ✧ Buttercup ✧ Molly Ringwald

Ultimate TV Trivia

Which Osbourne said, "I like the smell of armpits in the morning. It's like victory": Jack, Ozzy or Kelly?

On what late-night talk show did NFL football player Jason Sehorn propose to actress Angie Harmon?

During adventures on the cartoon *Dora the Explorer*™, viewers help Dora make decisions by following the _____ on the television screen.

HBO's *Project Greenlight* is based on a screenwriting competition hosted by which two Oscar®-winning writers?

Answers: ❖ Ozzy ❖ *The Tonight Show with Jay Leno* ❖ Cursor (as if the television were a computer) ❖ Matt Damon and Ben Affleck

Ultimate TV Trivia™

Which sitcom character's catch phrase is, "Don't be ridiculous": Alf (*ALF*), Mork (*Mork & Mindy*) or Balki (*Perfect Strangers*)?

- - - - - - -

In what rock star band did bandleader Max Weinburg play the drums before his stint on *Late Night with Conan O'Brien*?

- - - - - - -

On every episode of *Blue's Clues*™, Blue leaves clues for Steve or Joe by marking them with a _____ _____.

- - - - - - -

Which movie star got kicked off the set of *Romper Room* for bad behavior: Johnny Depp, Leonardo DiCaprio or Sean Penn?

Answers: ❖ Balki ❖ The E Street Band (with Bruce Springsteen) Paw print ❖ Leonardo DiCaprio (He was five years old.)

❖ 133 ❖

Ultimate TV Trivia

Who Said That?

Who on *Cheers* said, "If you can't say something nice, say it about Diane"?

Where Did It Happen?

Where do you enter when you listen and watch *The O'Reilly Factor* with Bill O'Reilly?

Blankety Blanks

The title characters on both *Crossing Jordan* and *Quincy, M.E.* work with _____ people.

TV Life Real Life

Which sitcom star did *not* marry his sitcom girlfriend: Michael J. Fox, Kirk Cameron or Scott Baio?

Ultimate TV Trivia™

 Which Griffin family member on *Family Guy* said, "Yo, did y'all check me when that hottie was all up in my Kool-Aid®": Stewie, Chris or Brian?

 What type of business does Ronnie, played by Kirstie Alley, own and manage on *Veronica's Closet*?

 On the '60s show *It Takes a Thief*, Noah Bain hires Alexander Mundy to work for the __ __ __.

 Is Patty Duke's real first name Mary Beth, Lily Ann or Anna Marie?

Answers: ❖ Chris ❖ A lingerie company ❖ SIA (a government spy agency) ❖ Anna Marie

Ultimate TV Trivia™

Who Said That?

Which *CSI* character said, "We already know she cooks like I do: takeout on speed dial": Gil Grissom, Sara Sidle or Catherine Willows?

—————————————

Where Did It Happen?

In what state does *Northern Exposure* take place?

—————————————

Blankety Blanks

Former model Brooke Burke hosts _____ ___ on the E! Entertainment Channel.

—————————————

TV Life Real Life

On what two TV shows did Frank Cady play Sam Drucker in the 1970s?

Ultimate TV Trivia™

Which sitcom husband said, "Honey, you may not have noticed this because I was so quiet...but I was sleeping": Paul (*Mad About You*), Al (*Married ... with Children*) or Ray (*Everybody Loves Raymond*)?

What is the final destination of the first *Amazing Race*?

Talk show host Sally Jessy Raphael is rarely seen without her trademark red _____.

Which show's soundtrack reached #1 on the '80s pop charts: *Knight Rider*, *St. Elsewhere* or *Miami Vice*?

Answers: ✧ Paul ✧ New York City (Flushing Meadows) ✧ Eyeglasses ✧ *Miami Vice*

Ultimate TV Trivia™

Which Cleaver family member on *Leave It to Beaver* said, "If it weren't for Eddie, who would we blame Wally's faults on": June, Ward or Beaver?

———————————

Where does the Western drama *Deadwood* take place?

———————————

On his late night show, Johnny Carson ends each of his monologues by performing a _____ _____.

———————————

What television host got his big break through a lawsuit involving the beef industry?

Answers: ❧ June ❧ The Black Hills, South Dakota ❧ Golf swing ❧ Dr. Phil McGraw

Ultimate TV Trivia

Who Said That?

On what show do audiences hear, "My dear guests, I am Mr. Roarke, your host"?

———————

Where Did It Happen?

What is the name of the restaurant where characters on the comedy *Alice* work?

———————

Blankety Blanks

After every monologue on her talk show, _____ _____ will dance before sitting down.

———————

TV Life Real Life

The stairs leading to which TV host's burial site display the words, "And Away We Go": Liberace (*The Liberace Show*), Jackie Gleason (*The Jackie Gleason Show*) or Milton Berle (*The Milton Berle Show*)?

Answers: ❧ *Fantasy Island* ❧ Mel's Diner ❧ Ellen DeGeneres ❧ Jackie Gleason

Ultimate TV Trivia

What '60s show's theme song includes the words, "People yakkity-yak a streak and waste your time of day"?

On what show do kids tune in to see Grandfather Clock, Orville the Dragon and Mr. Moose?

The original bandleader on *The Tonight Show with Jay Leno* was _____ _____.

Chris Henchy, a writer of *I'm with Her*, loosely based the show on his real-life romance with which famous actress?

Answers: ✦ *Mister Ed* ✦ Captain Kangaroo ✦ Branford Marsalis ✦ Brooke Shields

Ultimate TV Trivia

What game show host said, "You, Brian, may be within mere moments of committing the ultimate sin – winning all $5,000 of my money"?

What dating show starts out on a bus that has its own make-out room?

Lisa Ling replaced Debbie Matenopoulos on the talk show
_____ _____ .

Which sitcom star was married six times to four different women, marrying two of the same women twice: Freddie Prinze Sr., Fred Berry or Redd Foxx?

Answers: ☆ Ben Stein ☆ The 5th Wheel ☆ The View
☆ Fred Berry (Rerun from What's Happening!!)

Ultimate TV Trivia

 The theme song to which sitcom includes the words, "And in my opinionation, the sun is gonna surely shine": *Blossom*, *Growing Pains* or *Boy Meets World*?

_ _ _ _ _ _ _ _ _

 What high school do the students on *Saved by the Bell* attend?

_ _ _ _ _ _ _ _ _

 Jane Pauley, Stone Phillips, Tom Brokaw and Maria Shriver are news reporters for NBC's _____.

_ _ _ _ _ _ _ _ _

 What is the name given to the comedic puppet featured on the dance-themed show *Solid Gold*?

Answers: ✷ *Blossom* ✷ Bayside High School ✷ *Dateline* ✷ Madame

Ultimate TV Trivia

Who Said That?

What 1950s Disney™ TV movie character said, "Skipperdee is my turtle. He eats raisins. The Plaza is the only hotel in New York that will allow you to have a turtle."

——————————

Where Did It Happen?

At which university did Charles Van Doren teach before he became a contestant on *Twenty-One*?

——————————

Blankety Blanks

Cooking show host Jamie Oliver is better known to his viewers as the _____ _____.

——————————

TV Life Real Life

The plane seen on each episode of what TV show was previously owned by Richard D. Bach, author of *Jonathan Livingston Seagull*?

Answers: ❖ Eloise ❖ Columbia University ❖ Naked Chef ❖ Fantasy Island

Ultimate TV Trivia

Who Said That?

Which reality star made the two words, "You're fired!" a national catch phrase?

_ _ _ _ _ _ _ _

Where Did It Happen?

CNN broadcast headquarters are in what city?

_ _ _ _ _ _ _ _

Blankety Blanks

At the beginning of every episode of *The Daily Show*, the announcer states the full _____.

_ _ _ _ _ _ _ _

TV Life Real Life

Which of these actresses never played an "Angel" on *Charlie's Angels*: Shelley Hack, Priscilla Barnes or Tanya Roberts?

Answers: ❖ Donald Trump ❖ Atlanta ❖ Date (month, day, year) ❖ Priscilla Barnes (She played Terri on *Three's Company*.)

Ultimate TV Trivia™

Which single female said, "So all I have to do to meet the ideal man is give birth to him": Rachel (*Friends*), Miranda (*Sex and the City*) or Murphy (*Murphy Brown*)?

In what southwestern city did Dan Rather begin his career as a reporter?

The first episode of FOX's *24* shows David Palmer, who holds the office of _____, running for US president.

Who was the youngest member of the Osmonds on *The Osmond Family Show*?

Ultimate TV Trivia™

On what show is the following quote heard: "He basically called me white trash; he said I was from Riverside": *The O.C.*, *Buffy the Vampire Slayer* or *Beverly Hills, 90210*?

In what city does *Homicide: Life on the Streets* take place?

Nash Bridges drives a '71 _____ Barracuda convertible.

On which detective series was Agent 99 originally named Agent 69 until sponsors ordered the name changed?

Ultimate TV Trivia™

Who Said That?
On what show does designer Hildi say, "Everyone in America knows that I can rip up this carpet if I want to"?

__ __ __ __ __ __ __

Where Did It Happen?
Where does the TV drama *Law and Order: Special Victims Unit* take place?

__ __ __ __ __ __ __

Blankety Blanks
Jim on *According to Jim* plays in a _____ band in his garage.

__ __ __ __ __ __ __

TV Life Real Life
Which actor left the cast of *Eight is Enough* to work on *Star Wars*?

Ultimate TV Trivia

On what detective show can you hear the quote, "I don't want to live in a world where a person can't comb through another person's mail": *CSI: Miami*, *Monk* or *L.A. Dragnet*?

_._._._._._._

Name the city where the drama *Third Watch* takes place.

_._._._._._._

Dick Clark was in his _____ when he became host of *American Bandstand*.

_._._._._._._

In the '80s drama *Knight Rider*, was the voice of the car K.I.T.T. a female or a male?

Ultimate TV Trivia

Which sci-fi character said, "Unidentified Flying Objects. I think that fits the description pretty well. Tell me I'm crazy"?

_ _ _ _ _ _ _ _ _

On *The Ellen Degeneres Show*, where do guests who are unable to get a seat in the audience go to watch the show?

_ _ _ _ _ _ _ _ _

The show _____ _____ starring Dana Delaney won Emmys and a Golden Globe for its depiction of Vietnam in 1967.

_ _ _ _ _ _ _ _ _

On *Frasier*, what breed of dog is Eddie, played by a dog named Moose?

Answers: ❖ Fox Mulder ❖ The riff-raff room ❖ *China Beach*
❖ A Jack Russell terrier

Ultimate TV Trivia

Which *Everybody Loves Raymond* character said, "You called the teacher mommy? Why, was the teacher yelling": Ray, Robert or Frank?

——— ——— ——— ———

On the drama *American Dreams*, for which TV show does Meg dream of dancing?

——— ——— ——— ———

On *Early Edition*, Gary Hobson tries to stop disasters by reading the _____ ____-_____ each morning.

——— ——— ——— ———

Claire Danes got her TV acting start by landing the lead role on what drama?

Ultimate TV Trivia

Which FOX character often says, "I'm gonna kill one of them kids"?

—————————

On what show can viewers see a shot of the New York City restaurant El Teddy's during the opening credits: *The Late Show with David Letterman*, *Saturday Night Live* or *Jimmy Kimmel Live*?

—————————

Ken Wahl's character on the '80s drama *Wiseguy* wrestles with his morals while working as a/an _____ agent.

—————————

Which *Will & Grace* cast member composes music and is an accomplished pianist: Sean Hayes (Jack), Eric McCormack (Will) or Shelley Morrison (Rosario)?

Answers: ❖ Bernie Mac ❖ *Saturday Night Live* ❖ FBI ❖ Sean Hayes

Ultimate TV Trivia

What TV heroine said, "Do you remember that demon that almost got out the night I died"?

_·_·_·_·_·_·_

In which US city does the series *The Guardian* take place: Boston, Pittsburgh or Philadelphia?

_·_·_·_·_·_·_

In *Head of the Class,* teacher Billy MacGregor's accent originates from _____.

_·_·_·_·_·_·_

What 20-something movie actress provides the voice for Luanne on *King of the Hill*?

Answers: ❖ Buffy the Vampire Slayer ❖ Pittsburgh ❖ Scotland ❖ Brittany Murphy

Ultimate TV Trivia™

Who on *That '70s Show* said, "Fez, the foundation of every good relationship is three words: I don't know": Donna, Eric or Kelso?

Crossing Jordan is based in which east coast city: Boston, Providence or Hartford?

On *The Avengers*, John Steed's second female partner, _____ _____, often wears skin-tight one-piece outfits.

Which *Whose Line Is It Anyway?* regular (also the only cast member not to have a recurring role on *The Drew Carey Show*) went on to host a talk show?

Answers: ❖ Kelso ❖ Boston ❖ Emma Peel ❖ Wayne Brady

Ultimate TV Trivia™

"They can act, but can they bluff?" is the tagline for what show?

— — — — — — — — — —

On what game show do contestants enter The Winner's Circle in the last round of the game: *The Price is Right*, *Pyramid* or *Joker's Wild*?

— — — — — — — — — —

Paul Sorvino, who played Detective Phil Cerreta, left the cast of *Law & Order* after two seasons because outdoor filming in blustery weather was bad for his _____.

— — — — — — — — — —

What artist gained instant fame by singing the theme song for *Ally McBeal* and appearing as a regular on the show?

Answers: *Celebrity Poker* ❖ *Pyramid*
Throat (He has an operatic singing voice.) ❖ Vonda Shepard

Ultimate TV Trivia™

Which variety show host says, "Wunnerful, wunnerful": Steve Allen, Lawrence Welk or Jackie Gleason?

___ ___ ___ ___ ___ ___

What type of business does Mr. McFeely manage and own on *Mr. Roger's Neighborhood*?

___ ___ ___ ___ ___ ___

In the detective series starring Stephanie Zimbalist and Pierce Brosnan, the title of every episode contained the word _____.

___ ___ ___ ___ ___ ___

"Funeral March for a Marionette" is the instrumental theme song to what famous mystery series?

Ultimate TV Trivia™

On what '90s sci-fi show can you hear the quote, "You are like some other kind of alien, with, like, the ability to look like Max with that beard and those...gray hairs"?

—— —— —— —— —— ——

On the second season of *Making the Band*, to what New York City borough does P. Diddy send the group to fetch him a late-night serving of cheesecake?

—— —— —— —— —— ——

The gastronomic horticulturist private detective who solved all his cases (but one) from the comfort of his own home is _____ _____.

—— —— —— —— —— ——

Name the radio personality who supplies the voice for Norville "Shaggy" Rogers on *Scooby Doo*.

Ultimate TV Trivia™

Which character on *Saved by the Bell* said, "Be kind to geeks, nerds and dweebs. Ten years from now, they'll be the ones with all the money": Zack, A.C. or Screech?

The headquarters for *America's Most Wanted* are located in what city?

The title character of *McCloud* is a New Mexico cop on special assignment with the _____ _____ Police Department who retains his folksy Western ways.

Before Melissa Joan Hart became *Sabrina, the Teenage Witch*, she explained it all on what Nickelodeon™ comedy?

Ultimate TV Trivia

Which show's leading lady said, "I was over Jack way before he was over me and now he's moving on first? It's wrong. It's just wrong": *Suddenly Susan*, *Caroline in the City* or *Less Than Perfect*?

On what planet does the Jetson family live?

_____ ___ ___ is set in San Francisco, where a chief of police husband-and-wife team solves crimes with assistance from their housekeeper.

What is the name of the short-lived ABC series that was billed as a modern-day take on the classic *Dragnet*?

Answers: ❖ *Suddenly Susan* ❖ Earth (in the late 21st century) ❖ *McMillan and Wife* ❖ *L.A. Dragnet*

Ultimate TV Trivia

Who said, "I didn't want anyone to feel stress so I abandoned the traditional grading system and gave everyone happy faces": Dick (*3rd Rock from the Sun*), Charlie (*Head of the Class*) or Mr. Belding (*Saved by the Bell*)?

—————————————————

To what European city does Sabrina the Teenage Witch travel in a 1998 made-for-TV movie?

—————————————————

Martin Sheen plays the President of the United States on

_____ _____ _____.

—————————————————

What comedian was the voice of six characters on the cartoon *Fat Albert*?

Answers: ❖ Dick ❖ Rome (*Sabrina Goes to Rome*) ❖ *The West Wing* ❖ Bill Cosby

Ultimate TV Trivia

On which drama are the terms "Can Man," "Nozzle Man," "MVA" and "MPO" used: *Chicago Hope*, *Third Watch* or *Picket Fences*?

Freshmen Laura and Patty attend Weemawee High School on what '80s show?

On the sci-fi drama *Dark Angel*, main character Max was genetically engineered as a child and is now in hiding while working for a _____ _____.

The '60s show *Gidget* features what young actress, who is now an Oscar® winner?

Answers: ✵ *Third Watch* (The terms are firefighting terms.) ✵ *Square Pegs* ✵ Messenger service ✵ Sally Field

Ultimate TV Trivia™

Who said, "If you were more in touch with your feelings, you would be molesting them": a character on *Charles in Charge*, *thirtysomething* or *Get Smart*?

On what show did audiences see a man catching a bullet between his teeth and an acrobat leaping over speeding cars: *Ripley's Believe It or Not* or *That's Incredible*?

The dramatic sci-fi series *The Dead Zone* is based on the novel by _____ _____.

What CBS soap is the longest-running drama series on television?

Answers: ❖ *thirtysomething* (Gary) ❖ *That's Incredible*
❖ Stephen King ❖ *Guiding Light*

Ultimate TV Trivia™

Which *Dallas* star said to his estranged wife, "Go to bed Sue Ellen. There's nothing uglier than a woman who can't handle her liquor"?

What television show is taped live from the MTV studios overlooking Times Square?

On ____ _____, British Agent Steed cures a hangover with a concoction he calls the National Anthem.

Name *The Sopranos* actor who stars as FBI agent Joe Renato on *The Handler*.

Answers: ⁙ J.R. Ewing (Larry Hagman) ⁙ *Total Request Live* ⁙ *The Avengers* ⁙ Joe Pantoliano

Ultimate TV Trivia

What classic TV show's theme song includes the line, "But they're cousins, identical cousins all the way"?

_ . _ . _ . _ . _ . _ .

In what restaurant would you find the characters of *Beverly Hills, 90210* enjoying a burger or shake?

_ . _ . _ . _ . _ . _ .

The letters in the title of the prime time drama *CSI* stand for _____ _____ _____.

_ . _ . _ . _ . _ . _ .

What does the "Five-O" in *Hawaii Five-0* stand for?

Crime Scene Investigation ❖ The 50th state in the union

Answers: ❖ *The Patty Duke Show* ❖ The Peach Pit

❖ 163 ❖

Ultimate TV Trivia

What desert islander said, "I don't know how we're going to explain to our friends that we spent several years with people who aren't even in the social register"?

---·---·---·---·---

What 1876 mining town does HBO bring to life in a series starring Keith Carradine as Wild Bill?

---·---·---·---·---

On *JAG*, Lt. Harmon Rabb is a former Navy pilot who works as a _____.

---·---·---·---·---

Clint Eastwood got his big break when he was cast as Rowdy Yates in what classic western TV series?

Ultimate TV Trivia™

Who Said That?

Which *Sesame Street* character says, "My cute little eyes hear a cry for help" in his "Super" form?

Where Did It Happen?

What bar do the men of *The Sopranos* visit to see Silvio Dante and his exotic dancers?

Blankety Blanks

The drama *Third Watch* features a group of men and woman who work primarily as police officers, paramedics and _____.

TV Life Real Life

Grammy winner Mike Post composed the theme songs for *Hill Street Blues*, *L.A. Law*, and which other TV drama: *NYPD Blue*, *Cagney and Lacey* or *St. Elsewhere*?

Answers: ❖ Grover (as Super Grover) ❖ The Bada Bing ❖ Firemen ❖ *NYPD Blue*

Ultimate TV Trivia

Who Said That?

A character on which show said, "I know the German word for constipation, which I believe is 'farfrompoopin'": *Caroline in the City*, *Spin City* or *Sex and the City*?

Where Did It Happen?

In what US city do the lawyers on *The Practice* work?

Blankety Blanks

On _____ _____, two teams of homeowners have two days to redecorate each other's homes using a $1,000 budget per team.

TV Life Real Life

Jimmy Kimmel Live aired its premiere episode immediately after what sporting event?

Answers: ❖ *Spin City* (Mike) ❖ Boston ❖ *Trading Spaces* ❖ The Super Bowl

Ultimate TV Trivia™

Who on *NewsRadio* said, "I did not get into this business to make photocopies on just plain white paper. I just didn't": Joe, Beth or Matthew?

_____

What is the street address for *Sesame Street*?

_____

Steve Watson hosts _____ *House*, a show on which families vacate their homes for one week while a construction crew uniquely and substantially renovates their home.

_____

What stand-up comedian was an executive producer for *The Hughleys*, a sitcom about a black family living in a white suburb?

Ultimate TV Trivia™

On *Laverne & Shirley,* who said, "I woulda worn my tuxedo but my polo pony ate it": Carmine, Lenny or Squiggy?

On what network can viewers watch *True Hollywood Story,* an Emmy-nominated documentary series about Hollywood stars and their secrets?

Monica Lewinsky helped one hopeful woman find a new man when she hosted ____ _____ on FOX.

Which character did Regis Philbin play when he guest starred on Kelly Ripa's sitcom *Hope and Faith*: a used car salesman, a plumber or a choir director?

Answers: ❖ Squiggy ❖ E! Entertainment Television Network ❖ *Mr. Personality* ❖ A used car salesman

Ultimate TV Trivia™

What public figure said in a TV interview, "There were three of us in this marriage, so it was a bit crowded"?

Which west coast state is home to the town of Twin Peaks, featured on the TV show bearing the same name?

_____, a spin-off of _____, is the most successful and longest running television spin-off to date, earning its star three Emmys between 1993 and 2003.

Name the revamped network that popped up in 2003 and tagged itself as "America's network for men."

Ultimate TV Trivia

Who Said That?

On what show was the question, "Moose burger or caribou dog?" asked: *Due South*, *Northern Exposure* or *The Magnificent Seven*?

Where Did It Happen?

Where does Edith Ann, played by Lily Tomlin, sit as she talks to the audience on *Laugh-In*?

Blankety Blanks

Animated characters Mr. Peabody and Sherman use the _____ _____ when they want to travel in time.

TV Life Real Life

Which talk show host was once an Indiana TV weatherman: Howard Stern, David Letterman or Jay Leno?

Ultimate TV Trivia™

 Name the *Mad TV* character who says, "Look what I can do."

_ _ _ _ _ _ _ _ _ _

 Where does Tattoo on *Fantasy Island* go to get a better look at arriving planes?

_ _ _ _ _ _ _ _ _ _

 America's Funniest Home Videos features a segment called the _____ ____, which airs censored tapes.

_ _ _ _ _ _ _ _ _ _

 What Best Supporting Actress Oscar®-winner got her start playing Denise Huxtable's roommate Maggie on *A Different World*?

Answers: ❖ Stewart ❖ The bell tower ❖ Naughty File ❖ Marisa Tomei

Ultimate TV Trivia

Who on *Just Shoot Me* said, "I don't want you to lie – just have some fun with the truth": Elliot, Dennis or Jack?

- - - - - - - - - - -

On what island does *Wings* take place?

- - - - - - - - - - -

_____ _____ makes the Statue of Liberty disappear on one of his TV specials.

- - - - - - - - - - -

Benson's Katie Gatling and *Growing Pain*'s Carol Seaver are real life sisters, Missy and Tracey. What last name do they share?

Ultimate TV Trivia

A character from which show said, "You think wisdom is a flower for you to pluck. It is a mountain and it must be climbed": *Kung Fu*, *Martial Law* or *The Pretender*?

Where does Punky Brewster's mother abandon her when she is eight years old?

Dom DeLuise, Peter Funt, Suzanne Somers and Dina Eastwood were all hosts of _____ _____.

Rob Barnett and Jon Beckerman, creators of the comedy *Ed*, have also written for what late-night talk show?

Ultimate TV Trivia™

Who on *The Practice* said, "You think it's tough defending the guilty? Try the innocent – it's terrifying": Bobby Donnell, Jimmy Bertuli or Ellenor Frutt?

On *Gunsmoke*, where does Doc Adams go to buy a drink and pass the time?

Doogie on *Doogie Howser, M.D.* has been a doctor since the age of _____.

Name the cartoon that is the longest running original program in Nickelodeon™'s history.

Ultimate TV Trivia™

Which crime fighter said, "Sometimes we beat the system and sometimes it beats us": Nash Bridges, Matlock or Magnum, P.I.?

_._._._._._._._._

Describe the type of store where Walter, Maude's husband on *Maude*, works.

_._._._._._._._._

The show ____ _____ ____ _____ follows the life of a cartoonist whose popular children's book character is called Cosmic Cow.

_._._._._._._._._

The popularity of former Playboy model Jenny McCarthy soared after she landed a role on what MTV game show?

Ultimate TV Trivia

Who on *Dragnet* says, "Just the facts, ma'am"?

___ ___ ___ ___ ___

Do the events on *McHale's Navy* take place in the Virgin Islands, South Pacific Islands or Hawaiian Islands?

___ ___ ___ ___ ___

The sitcom *Alice* is based on the 1974 Scorsese film, *Alice* _____ _____ _____ _____, starring Ellen Burstyn.

___ ___ ___ ___ ___

Which *Fame* came first: the movie or the TV series?

Answers: ❖ Sergeant Joe Friday ❖ South Pacific Islands (Taratupa) ❖ *Doesn't Live Here Anymore* ❖ The movie

❖ 176 ❖

Ultimate TV Trivia™

Who on *The Dukes of Hazzard* said to Bosco, "If brains was watermelons you wouldn't have enough seeds to fill a tin": Daisy Duke, Luke Duke or Boss Hogg?

The military characters on what show keep camp at Stalag 13?

During the 1950s, the _____ _____ _____ featured "Talent Round-Up Day" every Friday.

What '80s drama stars *The Six Million Dollar Man*?

Ultimate TV Trivia™

 Who on *Dharma and Greg* said, "Ha, you try to cry when you're eating pudding, I dare you": Dharma or Greg?

_._._._._._._

 Name the TV program on which Tim and Al of *Home Improvement* demonstrate home decoration and repair tips.

_._._._._._._

 The Palm Beach detective team of Lance and Lorenzo, played by Rob Estes and Mitzi Kapture, fights crime on _____ _____.

_._._._._._._

 Name the longest running and most watched detective series in American TV history.

Ultimate TV Trivia™

Which *60 Minutes* correspondent asks the question, "Did you ever notice"?

————————————

Martha Stewart Living is broadcast from Martha's studio located in which state?

————————————

Franchelle "Frenchie" Davis was kicked off _____ _____ __ for posing nude on an adult website before becoming a contestant on the show.

————————————

Susan Dey, also known as *The Partridge Family's* Laurie, practiced law on what TV program?

Ultimate TV Trivia

Which *Academy Awards*® host said, "I'm a sucker for a free tuxedo"?

_ _ _ _ _ _ _ _

What is the name of the beer company where Laverne and Shirley work?

_ _ _ _ _ _ _ _

Hayden Fox is the head coach for a college _____ team on the sitcom *Coach*.

_ _ _ _ _ _ _ _

Which television network did kids rush home to watch for its *Afterschool Special* series, which mixed education with entertainment?

Answers: ✧ Billy Crystal (1998) ✧ Shotz Brewery (*Laverne & Shirley*) ✧ Football ✧ ABC

Ultimate TV Trivia

Who on *M*A*S*H* says, "bull cookies" and "sweet limburger": Colonel Sherman Potter, Major Margaret Houlihan or Corporal Radar O'Reilly?

Name the Arizona fort where Rusty and his German shepherd Rin Tin Tin live.

Trapper John of *Trapper John, M.D.* is the _____ _____ _____ at San Francisco Memorial Hospital.

Which pop singer appeared on the '70s sitcoms *Good Times* and *Diff'rent Strokes*?

Ultimate TV Trivia

Who said, "Heeeere's Johnny!" on *The Tonight Show with Johnny Carson*?

__ __ __ __ __ __

On *The Arsenio Hall Show*, what is the area called where audience members stand and "woof"?

__ __ __ __ __ __

On *South Park*, Cartman's favorite junk food snack is

_____ _____.

__ __ __ __ __ __

Who are Salvatore and Cherilyn better known as?

Ultimate TV Trivia™

The leading man on which show said, "Somebody always shoots at us when we're kissing": *Hart to Hart*, *Remington Steele* or *The Scarecrow and Mrs. King*?

What aspiring actress lives in Manhattan in apartment 4-D on West 78th Street?

My Big Fat _____ _____ is a reality show that tricks a family into thinking their planted future son-in-law is the real deal.

Goldie Hawn performed as a befuddled blonde character on what sketch comedy show?

Ultimate TV Trivia

Who said, "Been there, done that," in response to "Go to hell": Spike (*Buffy the Vampire Slayer*), Xena (*Xena: Warrior Princess*) or Angel (*Angel*)?

The title character on *Lovejoy* works at what type of retail shop?

The _____ network aired the Michael Jackson special in which Martin Bashir showed clips of his eight-month visit with the singer.

Which actor starred on both *Silver Spoons* and *The Fresh Prince of Bel-Air*?

Answers: ✧ Angel ✧ Antique ✧ ABC (as part of a 20/20 special) ✧ Alfonso Ribeiro

Ultimate TV Trivia

Which children's show started off with a voice yelling, "Hey, you guys!": *The New Zoo Revue*, *The Electric Company* or *Romper Room*?

What is the name of the bar that Archie owns in the spin-off of *All in the Family*?

Michael Flaherty is the _____ _____ of New York City in *Spin City*.

The *King of Queens'* Leah Remini got her TV start on the short-lived *Living Dolls*, a spin-off of which '80s sitcom?

Ultimate TV Trivia

Who on *Full House* says, "How rude": Stephanie, Michelle or Jesse?

_._._._._._._._

The heroes of what show fight evil lawyers at the firm Wolfram & Hart?

_._._._._._._._

The call letters of the radio station on *Newsradio* are __ __ __ __.

_._._._._._._._

Name two of the soaps that Rick Springfield appeared on before landing a number one hit with *Jessie's Girl*.

Ultimate TV Trivia™

On *Laugh-In*, who plays the German soldier who says, "very interesting": Henry Gibson, Dennis Allen or Arte Johnson?

Do the *Desperate Housewives* live on Poinsettia Street, Daffodil Drive or Wisteria Lane?

World leader _____ _____ invites the Simpson family over to his house for tea after they deplane in his country.

Did *The Smurfs* win an Emmy for Outstanding Animated Program in 1975, 1982 or 1988?

Answers: ❖ Arte Johnson ❖ Wisteria Lane ❖ Tony Blair (*The Simpsons*) ❖ 1982

Ultimate TV Trivia™

Which TV heroes say, "It's morphin' time"?

_ _ _ _ _ _ _

Describe the type of factory where George of *George Lopez* works in Los Angeles.

_ _ _ _ _ _ _

The classic series *Love*, _____ _____ shows how people of different walks of life find love.

_ _ _ _ _ _ _

Which sitcom wife sang backup for Bob Dylan, Bette Midler and Tanya Tucker: Patricia Richardson (*Home Improvement*), Katey Sagal (*8 Simple* Rules) or Patricia Heaton (*Everybody Loves Raymond*)?

Answers: ❖ Mighty Morphin Power Rangers ❖ It is an airplane parts factory. ❖ *American Style* ❖ Katey Sagal

Ultimate TV Trivia™

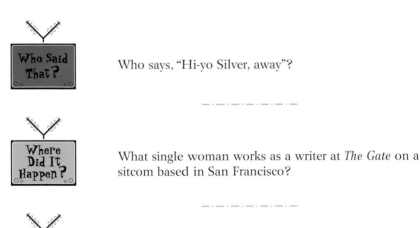

Who Said That?

Who says, "Hi-yo Silver, away"?

_. _ . _ . _ . _ . _ . _

Where Did It Happen?

What single woman works as a writer at *The Gate* on a sitcom based in San Francisco?

_. _ . _ . _ . _ . _ . _

Blankety Blanks

Tim Russert is the host and moderator of _____ _____ _____, TV's most popular Sunday morning news show.

_. _ . _ . _ . _ . _ . _

TV Life Real Life

What Latino singing sensation landed a role as Miguel Morez on *General Hospital*?

Answers: ❖ The Lone Ranger ❖ Susan Keane (*Suddenly Susan*) ❖ *Meet the Press* ❖ Ricky Martin

Ultimate TV Trivia™

Portraying Reggie Van Gleason, the host of which show says, "Mmmmmm boy, that's good booze": *The Dean Martin Show*, *The Jackie Gleason Show* or *The Red Skelton Show*?

———————————

The theme song to *Car 54, Where Are You?* refers to a hold up in which NYC borough?

———————————

Emergency! follows the lives of squad members assigned to Engine number ____.

———————————

Jennifer Aniston's real-life father, John Aniston, portrays Victor Kiriakis on what popular TV soap?

Ultimate TV Trivia

Who on *Batman* says, "holy guacamole" and "holy ravioli": Batman, Robin or Alfred?

_ _ _ _ _ _ _ _

In what city does *CSI: Crime Scene Investigation's* crime team uncover the truth?

_ _ _ _ _ _ _ _

Mr. Lipshultz is a _____ teacher on *Boston Public*.

_ _ _ _ _ _ _ _

Which actor was the original operator for the "Picture Picture" segment on *Mister Rogers' Neighborhood*: Robin Williams, Michael Keaton or Jim Belushi?

Answers: ❖ Robin ❖ Las Vegas ❖ History ❖ Michael Keaton

❖ 191 ❖

Ultimate TV Trivia

 Which western damsel says, "Be careful, Matt": Miss Kitty (*Gunsmoke*), Victoria (*The Big Valley*) or Linda (*High Chaparral*)?

 On *Friends*, Monica and Chandler secretly start seeing each other at Ross' wedding to Emily in what European city?

 The soap opera parody *Soap* takes place in and around the homes of the _____ and the _____.

 What Academy Award-nominated actor played characters like Easy Reader, Mark, Count Dracula and Mel Mounds the DJ on the popular children's series *Electric Company*?

Ultimate TV Trivia™

On which game show are contestants told by Groucho Marx to "say the secret word": *Dr. I.Q.*, *You Bet Your Life* or *Monkey Business*?

What super-human works for the Office of Scientific Intelligence?

On the dating show _____, a sexy single begins a date with four members of the opposite sex and ends up with the one of his or her choice.

John Stamos landed his first TV role as Blackie Parrish on which popular soap?

Ultimate TV Trivia

Who Said That?

Which kids' show host says, "Abracadabra, please and thank you": Mr. Rogers, Captain Kangaroo or Pee Wee Herman?

Where Did It Happen?

Is *8 Simple Rules for Dating My Teenage Daughter* based in Michigan, Ohio or Indiana?

Blankety Blanks

The History Channel and The Biography Channel are part of the larger _____ Television Networks company.

TV Life Real Life

Who starred as a crime-fighting teen on *21 Jump Street* before playing Edward Scissorhands in the Tim Burton flick?

Answers: ❖ Captain Kangaroo ❖ Michigan ❖ A&E ❖ Johnny Depp

Ultimate TV Trivia™

Who says, "Jane, stop this crazy thing!" at the end of each cartoon?

In the series finale of *Frasier,* Frasier Crane is offered a job in San Francisco but instead hops on a plane to which US city?

The History Channel's _____ _____ shows how notable institutions like the drive-thru restaurant and The Berlin Wall came to fruition.

Before starring on *The Scarecrow and Mrs. King* and *Charlie's Angels*, Kate Jackson played a cop's wife in what show?

Answers: ✧ George Jetson ✧ Chicago ✧ *Modern Marvels* ✧ *The Rookies*

Ultimate TV Trivia™

 Which of these '70s sitcom stars said, "Loo-king good": Chico (*Chico and the Man*), Dwayne (*What's Happening!!*) or J.J. (*Good Times*)?

 In the '70s drama *Emergency!*, the paramedics, fire and police departments worked together saving lives in what city?

 Futurama's Bender is a robot and Leela is a _____.

 Talk show ringmaster Jerry Springer was the mayor of what city: Cincinnati, Cleveland or St. Louis?

Ultimate TV Trivia™

What '70s series started out each episode by singing, "Na na na, gonna have a good time"?

_ . _ . _ . _

On *Family Affair*, Bill Davis' life is interrupted when his orphaned relatives come to live with him in his swanky bachelor pad located in what city?

_ . _ . _ . _

Max _____ is a computer-generated character who starred in a science fiction series bearing his name.

_ . _ . _ . _

Which TV host finished in the top ten of the 1970 Miss America pageant: Meredith Vieira, Kathie Lee Gifford or Mary Hart?

Answers: ❖ *Fat Albert and the Cosby Kids* ❖ New York ❖ Headroom (*Max Headroom*) ❖ Mary Hart (*Entertainment Tonight*)

Ultimate TV Trivia™

Which '60s sci-fi series included the lines, "There is nothing wrong with your television set. Do not attempt to adjust the picture": *The Outer Limits*, *The Twilight Zone* or *Tales from the Darkside*?

----·--·--·--·--·--

On *The Fresh Prince of Bel-Air*, where did Will Smith's character live before his mother sent him to live with his aunt and uncle?

----·--·--·--·--·--

In addition to serving their church, Father _____ and Sister _____ solved crimes on a TV mystery series.

----·--·--·--·--·--

Which news reporter was the *Today Show*'s first female co-host: Barbara Walters, Jane Pauley or Estelle Parsons?

Ultimate TV Trivia™

What TV horror series closes each episode with the narration, "Until next time, try to enjoy the daylight"?

_ _ _ _ _ _ _ _

The hilarious and often smutty humor of *The Benny Hill Show* was brought to America in the '70s from what country?

_ _ _ _ _ _ _ _

The full title of the sketch comedy show *Laugh-In* is _____ & _____'s *Laugh-In*.

_ _ _ _ _ _ _ _

Which former *Today Show* host received a Guinness World Record™ in 1985 for having recorded the most hours on commercial network television: Hugh Downs, Tom Brokaw or Mike Wallace?

Answers: ❖ *Tales from the Darkside* ❖ England ❖ *Rowan: Martin* ❖ Hugh Downs

Ultimate TV Trivia™

Who says, "Wocka, wocka wocka" on *The Muppet Show*?

_ _ _ _ _ _ _ _

What is the name of the fort where Capt. Wilton Parmenter is given command after accidentally being deemed a hero in *F- Troop*?

_ _ _ _ _ _ _ _

Three friends get into mischief at Principal Musso's Flamingo High School on _____ _____ *Can't Lose*.

_ _ _ _ _ _ _ _

Which of these newswomen became the first female co-anchor of TV's *60 Minutes*: Deborah Norville, Diane Sawyer or Jane Pauley?

Ultimate TV Trivia™

Which '70s police detective used to say, "Who loves ya, baby": Tony Baretta (*Baretta*), Theo Kojak (*Kojak*) or Linc Hayes (*The Mod Squad*)?

Where do grumpy police detective Phil Fish and his wife, Bernice, live while raising five rowdy foster children in the sitcom *Fish*?

The letters QVC on the QVC network stand for _____, _____ and Convenience.

Which talk show host permanently withdrew his/her name from Daytime Emmy Award consideration due to receiving the Lifetime Achievement recognition in 1998?

Ultimate TV Trivia™

Who Said That?

Which of these TV characters said, "Great Caesar's Ghost": Perry White (*Adventures of Superman*), Commissioner Gordon (*Batman*) or Major Steve Trevor (*Wonder Woman*)?

Where Did It Happen?

In what city do officers Pete Malloy and Jim Reed patrol the streets in the drama *Adam 12*?

Blankety Blanks

The letters ESPN stand for the _____ and _____ Network.

TV Life Real Life

Which talk show host announced in 1999 that he has multiple sclerosis?

Answers: ✧ Perry White ✧ Los Angeles ✧ Entertainment; Sports Programming ✧ Montel Williams

Ultimate TV Trivia

What '70s detective said, "Don't do the crime if you can't do the time"?

___ ___ ___ ___ ___ ___ ___

On which of these submarines did the '60s sci-fi drama *Voyage to the Bottom of the Sea* take place: Stingray, Sea Quest or Seaview?

___ ___ ___ ___ ___ ___ ___

The film _____ _____ was broadcast on NBC in 1997 with no commercial breaks except for two corporate messages from the Ford Motor Co.

___ ___ ___ ___ ___ ___ ___

Chicago Hope's Mark Harmon, who played Dr. Jack McNeil, also played a doctor on what hospital drama?

Schindler's List ❖ *St. Elsewhere*

Answers: ❖ Detective Tony Baretta (Robert Blake of *Baretta*) ❖ Seaview

Ultimate TV Trivia™

Who originally said, "Smile, you're on Candid Camera!" and was the inventor of television pranks: Bob Saget, Durward Kirby or Allen Funt?

On *My Favorite Martian*, reporter Timothy O'Hara rescues a Martian after his spaceship crashes near what city?

The mysterious character Don Diego de la Vero is better known by the name _____.

Which *Touched By An Angel* star gained fame by taking it *One Day at a Time*?

Ultimate TV Trivia™

Which character from *McHale's Navy* repeatedly asked, "What is it McHale? What do you want, what, what?": Capt. Binghamton, Ens. Charles Parker or Lt. Elroy Carpenter?

Where did the man of steel work as mild-mannered reporter Clark Kent in the *Adventures of Superman*?

In 1951, the _____ _____ company aired its first of many *Hall of Fame* television specials.

What name does the father/son team that runs New York's Orange County Choppers motorcycle shop on *American Choppers* share?

Answers: ❖ Captain Binghamton ❖ The Daily Planet ❖ Hallmark Cards (*Hallmark Hall of Fame*) ❖ Paul (Teutul)

Ultimate TV Trivia

Who Said That?

Which character from *The Addams Family* says, "You rang?"

_ _ _ _ _ _ _ _

Where Did It Happen?

On *The Flying Nun*, Sally Field plays Sister Bertrille, a nun who helps the community by using her ability to fly all around the San Tanco Convent, located on what island?

_ _ _ _ _ _ _ _

Blankety Blanks

The CBS drama *Joan* _____ _____ features Joan Osborne's controversial "One of Us" as its theme song.

_ _ _ _ _ _ _ _

TV Life Real Life

On MTV's *Punk'd*, Halle Berry is told there is no room for her at the premiere of which movie she stars in?

Answers: ✣ Lurch ✣ Puerto Rico ✣ *of Arcadia* ✣ *Gothika*

Ultimate TV Trivia™

Which character from *Hogan's Heroes* repeatedly said, "Dismissed": Colonel Klink, Sergeant Schultz or Colonel Hogan?

On *Melrose Place*, residents lived in what famous district of Los Angeles?

In The '60s series *The _____ and Mrs. _____,* Captain Daniel Gregg haunts a lovely young widow and her two children when they move into their New England seaside house.

Which *The Cosby Show* kid now has her own sitcom and is the voice for Kim on the cartoon *Kim Possible*?

Answers: ❖ Colonel Klink ❖ West Hollywood ❖ *Ghost; Muir* ❖ Raven-Symoné (Olivia)

Ultimate TV Trivia

Which famous comedian said, "Nice to be here? At my age it's nice to be anywhere": Jack Benny, Milton Berle or George Burns?

— — — — — — — — —

On what TV show can characters be found drinking beer at 112 ½ Beacon Street?

— — — — — — — — —

In the '60s series *The _____ of Eddie's Father*, little Eddie is always scheming to get his magazine publisher dad, Tom Corbett, married.

— — — — — — — — —

Which half of the *Laverne and Shirley* duo became a big-name Hollywood director?

Answers: ❖ George Burns ❖ *Cheers* ❖ *Courtship* ❖ Laverne (Penny Marshall)

Ultimate TV Trivia

What series theme song says, "Go right to the source and ask the horse, he'll give you the answer that you'll endorse"?

_____

On *The Munsters*, where did Eddie's pet dragon, Spot, live?

_____

On *Get Smart*, Maxwell Smart, Agent _____ often depends on his competent partner and best girl, Agent _____.

_____

Continuing his tradition of playing a crime fighter in a small Southern town, Andy Griffith starred as what aging attorney after his success in *The Andy Griffith Show*?

Answers: ❖ *Mister Ed* ❖ Under the stairs ❖ 86; 99 ❖ Benjamin Matlock (*Matlock*)

Ultimate TV Trivia

Who always says, "Yes, Master"?

_____

On *The Dick Van Dyke Show*, Laura and Rob Petrie live next to Millie and Jerry in what NYC suburb: New Rochelle, Yonkers or Larchmont?

_____

The 1965 TV series, *Please Don't _____ the _____* was based on the best-selling book and movie of the same name.

_____

What is the name of the *Dragnet* producer, star and frequent scriptwriter who based many of his episodes on actual L.A. Police Department cases?

Answers: ❖ Jeannie ❖ New Rochelle ❖ *Eat; Daisies* ❖ Jack Webb

Ultimate TV Trivia™

In his *Saturday Night Live* parody of *The Little Rascals* character Buckwheat, who sang "Wookin' Pa Nub" and "Fee Times a Mady"?

_ _ _ _ _ _ _ _ _ _ _

Nosy neighbor Gladys Kravits lives near which TV husband and wife?

_ _ _ _ _ _ _ _ _ _ _

Angie Dickenson starred as no-nonsense police Sergeant Suzanne "Pepper" Anderson in the '70s crime drama *Police* _____.

_ _ _ _ _ _ _ _ _ _ _

Which crime solver's character is based on Petrovich from Dostoevsky's *Crime and Punishment*: Kojak, Columbo or Maverick?

Answers: ❖ Eddie Murphy ❖ Samantha and Darrin Stephens (*Bewitched*) ❖ *Woman* ❖ Columbo

Ultimate TV Trivia

Who said, "It's fun to put it in, but then you have to fold it," when talking about laundry: Anna Nicole Smith (*The Anna Nicole Show*), Kelly Osbourne (*The Osbournes*) or Jessica Simpson (*Newlyweds*)?

Good Times was a '70s sitcom based on a poor African-American family and their life in the housing projects of what city?

Dr. David Bruce Banner is played by _____ _____ in the '70s series *The Incredible Hulk*.

What controversial documentary filmmaker hosted Bravo's *The Awful Truth*?

Answers: ✵ Jessica Simpson ✵ Chicago ✵ Bill Bixby ✵ Michael Moore

Ultimate TV Trivia™

Which *Smallville* character said, "You see, I don't want to do good things; I want to do great things": Clark Kent, Lana Lang or Lex Luther?

On *The Cosby Show*, in what country does Denise Huxtable get married?

Using artificial body parts giving her super powers, Jamie Sommers is the first female cyborg. She works undercover for the government while posing as a schoolteacher on the '70s series *The _____ _____*.

What future fashion plate played nerd Patty Greene on the short-lived sitcom *Square Pegs*?

Ultimate TV Trivia

 Before reading a clue to contestants, which game show host says, "And the answer is..."?

 On *Trading Spaces*, in what state does the two-hour "$100,000 Challenge" episode take place: California, Florida or Massachusetts?

 The classic series, *Hopalong Cassidy* followed Hoppie and his horse, _____ , catching bad guys across the West.

 Who on *The Practice* was named one of *People* magazine's Most Intriguing People of the Year: Camryn Manheim, James Spader or Steve Harris?

Ultimate TV Trivia™

What show's host says, "If you get it on tape, you could get it in cash"?

On *The Honeymooners*, where did Ralph Kramden always tell Alice he wanted to send her?

Officers Toody and Muldoon played a "Mutt and Jeff" policeman pair at the mythical 53rd precinct in the Bronx in the '60s comedy _____ _____, *Where Are You*?

Which member of The Beatles was the best man at Peter Boyle's (*Everybody Loves Raymond*) wedding?

Answers: ❖ *America's Funniest Home Videos* ❖ To the moon ❖ *Car 54* ❖ John Lennon

Ultimate TV Trivia

On which TV show does a character say, "I ate my eraser," while eating Chinese food with pencils instead of chopsticks: *Barney Miller, Whose Line Is It Anyway?* or *Welcome Back, Kotter*?

_._._._._._._

In what state does the sitcom *Coach* take place?

_._._._._._._

Best-known for throwing thousands of pies in his career, _____ _____ even nabbed the likes of stars like Frank Sinatra, Tony Curtis and Sammy Davis Jr. for his weekly television program.

_._._._._._._

Larry David, star of the HBO comedy *Curb Your Enthusiasm*, was the inspiration for which *Seinfeld* character?

Ultimate TV Trivia™

Which TV show's lyrics include the lines, "Believe it or not I'm walking on air; I never thought I could feel so free": *Wings*, *Designing Women* or *Greatest American Hero*?

On *The Love Boat*, where could you usually find Isaac?

"Faster than a _____ _____! More powerful than a _____! Able to leap tall buildings in a single bound!" was proclaimed in each episode of the *Adventures of Superman*.

Which former member of the TV comedy *Growing Pains* has six children: Alan Thicke, Kirk Cameron or Joanna Kearns?

Ultimate TV Trivia

On which TV show did a character say, "I'm allergic to microwaves. They release space hamsters into my bloodstream": *The A-Team*, *The X-Files* or *The Twilight Zone*?

The Tanner sisters live at 1882 Gerard Street with their dad and their Uncle Jesse on what TV show?

On the TV series *My _____ _____*, Uncle Martin's alien name is Exodus.

Who portrayed Jackie Templeton on *General Hospital* before landing big screen roles in '80s movies like *St. Elmo's Fire* and *About Last Night*?

Ultimate TV Trivia

On which TV show did Kermit the Frog say, "If you lick a frog, you were crazy to start with": *Sesame Street*, *The Muppet Show* or *The Daily Show*?

In an episode of the series *Quantum Leap*, the year is 1970 and Sam Beckett is a Navy Seal trying to save his brother's life in what country?

On *Family Affair*, Bill Davis takes care of his orphaned relatives with the help of his butler, Mr. _____.

Which comedy star co-owns the House of Blues club with Dan Aykroyd?

Ultimate TV Trivia™

Did Heathler Locklear say, "I'm not interested in your man, so why don't you just march those $12 pumps back to the trailer park" on *T.J. Hooker*, *Spin City* or *Dynasty*?

On *Murphy Brown*, in what city does Murphy work?

Dark _____ is a '60s gothic soap opera about a New England family and the horrific occurrences they encounter.

Which member of *Will & Grace* is the lead singer in the LA band, The Supreme Music Program: Debra Messing, Megan Mullally or Sean Hayes?

Answers: ❖ *Spin City* ❖ Washington, D.C. ❖ *Shadows* ❖ Megan Mullally

Ultimate TV Trivia

Who Said That?

What game show host said, "Keep your eye on this spot! You are about to see one celebrity and one contestant step into this circle with a chance to win $10,000 in less than a minute!"

Where Did It Happen?

What Manhattan-based courtroom comedy features Markie Post, Richard Moll and John Larroquette?

Blankety Blanks

The annual *Divas* concert, showcasing women musicians, is aired on _____.

TV Life Real Life

Which star worked for General Mills sweeping up Cheerios dust in his home town of Cedar Rapids, Iowa: Matt LeBlanc (*Friends*), Tracy Morgan (*The Tracy Morgan Show*) or Ashton Kutcher (*That '70s Show*)?

Answers: ✷ Dick Clark (*$10,000 Pyramid*) ✷ *Night Court* ✷ VH1 ✷ Ashton Kutcher

Ultimate TV Trivia™

On which TV show did Bill Cosby's character say, "If you're going to fly through the jungle like Superman, someone has to be there to carry your phone booth": *Kids Say the Darndest Things*, *The Cosby Show* or *I Spy*?

On the original *Star Trek* series, Captain James T. Kirk was born in what US state?

Before turning herself in to the CIA, Irena Derevko of *Alias* worked for the _____.

Which two *WKRP in Cincinnati* stars had a real life romance during the taping of the show?

Answers: ❖ *I Spy* ❖ Iowa ❖ KGB ❖ Loni Anderson and Gary Sandy (They played Jennifer and Andy.)

Ultimate TV Trivia

Who Said That?

"That's what you get for river dancing in a thong" is a quote from: *Whose Line Is It Anyway?*, *Ally McBeal* or *The Rosie O'Donnell Show*?

Where Did It Happen?

On *Charmed*, where do the three sisters find *The Book of Shadows* that they use to release their powers?

Blankety Blanks

The _____ channel uses the exclamation, "Oh!" as it's simple tagline.

TV Life Real Life

What actor became known as "King of the Miniseries," due to his star roles on *Shogun*, *Centennial* and *The Thorn Birds*?

Answers: ❖ *Whose Line Is It Anyway?* ❖ The attic ❖ Oxygen ❖ Richard Chamberlain

Ultimate TV Trivia

Who on *General Hospital* says, "As deep-fried as it may be, the girl has a heart": Justice Ward, Luke Spencer or Sonny Corinthos?

––– – ––– – ––– – –––

The 1979 debut of PBS's *This Old House* was based in what US state?

––– – ––– – ––– – –––

Deborah Norville is the host of the sensational journalism show_____ _____.

––– – ––– – ––– – –––

Fred Grandy, who later ran successfully for US Congress, played which character on the Love Boat?

Ultimate TV Trivia™

Who Said That?

Which TV show featured a police detective who often said, "Trust me, I know what I'm doing" even though the opposite was usually true: *Sledge Hammer!*, *Cagney & Lacey* or *Cop Rock*?

Where Did It Happen?

On *I Love Lucy*, what is the name of Ricky Ricardo's club?

Blankety Blanks

Comedienne _____ _____ took over Rosie O'Donnell's TV spot in 2002.

TV Life Real Life

What former '70s TV detective went by the name Mickey Gubitosi in the *Our Gang* comedies?

Answers: ✵ *Sledge Hammer!* ✵ The Tropicana ✵ Caroline Rhea (*The Caroline Rhea Show*) ✵ Robert Blake (*Baretta*)

✵ 225 ✵

Ultimate TV Trivia

"You wanna keep it down? I can't hear the war" is a line from: *M*A*S*H*, *China Beach* or *Band of Brothers*?

––– – –– ––– ––– ––– –

In what California city do the orphaned Salinger kids live on *Party of Five*?

––– – –– ––– ––– ––– –

On the drama _____, Swoozie Kurtz plays Alex, the eldest sister.

––– – –– ––– ––– ––– –

Cyndi Lauper won an Emmy Award for her guest appearance as Marianne, the ex-wife of which *Mad About You* character?

Answers: ❖ *China Beach* ❖ San Francisco ❖ *Sisters* ❖ Ira Buchman

Ultimate TV Trivia

Who on *The Odd Couple* says, "I like ketchup. It's like tomato wine": Murray, Felix or Oscar?

On *Magnum, P.I.*, Thomas Magnum was a Naval officer stationed at what US base before he became a detective?

The sitcom *Benson* was a spin-off of the popular sitcom _____.

Actor Van Williams as the Green Hornet teamed up with what martial arts master as Kato in the '60 series *The Green Hornet*?

Answers: ❖ Oscar ❖ Pearl Harbor ❖ *Soap* ❖ Bruce Lee

Ultimate TV Trivia

Which character on *The Dick Van Dyke Show* says, "I'm not angry with you. I'm angry with me for being angry with you": Laura Petrie, Sally Rogers or Millie Helper?

_ . _ . _ . _ . _ . _ . _

On *Make Room for Daddy*, Danny Thomas' character runs into Andy Taylor while traveling through which small town?

_ . _ . _ . _ . _ . _ . _

The dogs who played *Lassie* were all members of the _____ breed.

_ . _ . _ . _ . _ . _ . _

What *Nash Bridges* star also records bilingual children's albums?

Ultimate TV Trivia

"Look, it's his show. If he wants to be hard to kill, let him" is a quote from *The Bullwinkle Show*, *Mighty Mouse* or *Pinky and the Brain*?

-·-·-·-·-·-·-·-

In what city did Eliot Ness fight crime in *The Untouchables*?

-·-·-·-·-·-·-·-

_____ _____ was added to the cast of *Spin City* when Michael J. Fox left the sitcom.

-·-·-·-·-·-·-·-

Magnum, P.I. star Tom Selleck began his career in what occupation?

Answers: ❖ *The Bullwinkle Show* ❖ Chicago ❖ Charlie Sheen ❖ Modeling

❖ 229 ❖

Ultimate TV Trivia™

"The owls are not what they seem" is a line from *The X-Files*, *Charmed* or *Twin Peaks*?

___ ___ ___ ___ ___

On the show *Felicity*, Felicity Porter goes to college at what fictional east-coast school?

___ ___ ___ ___ ___

Glenn Fry's song "_____ _____" inspired an episode (in which he also guest-starred) of the '90s drama *Miami Vice*.

___ ___ ___ ___ ___

Which actress portrayed Audrey Hepburn in the made for TV movie *The Audrey Hepburn Story*?

Answers: ✣ *Twin Peaks* ✣ UNY (University of New York) ✣ *Smuggler's Blues* ✣ Jennifer Love Hewitt

✣ 230 ✣

Ultimate TV Trivia™

Which cartoon character said, "This looks like a job for the Masked Avenger...but since he's not around, I guess I'll have to do it": Daffy Duck, Elmer Fudd or Bugs Bunny?

_ . _ . _ . _ . _ . _

In which state is *Dawson's Creek* filmed: Michigan, Georgia or North Carolina?

_ . _ . _ . _ . _ . _

Game show personality Chuck Woolery was the host of _____ _____ _____ before Pat Sajak.

_ . _ . _ . _ . _ . _

Which *Falcon Crest* star was married to Ronald Reagan during the 1940s?

Ultimate TV Trivia

Who on *The Andy Griffith Show* said, "If there's anything that upsets me, it's having people say I'm sensitive": Goober Pyle, Floyd Lawson or Barney Fife?

On *Judging Amy*, Amy Brenneman is a single mother who left New York to become a family court judge in what state?

Curb Your Enthusiasm's Larry David is the co-creator of the popular sitcom _____.

What is the name of the prolific producer behind *Ally McBeal* and *The Practice* who is married to Michelle Pfeiffer?

Ultimate TV Trivia

Who Said That?

What TV detective said, "I'll tell you how you did it if you're interested"?

Where Did It Happen?

Which TV show featured two men in drag living at the Susan B. Anthony Hotel?

Blankety Blanks

Before starring on *Scrubs*, Sarah Chalke played Becky from 1993 to 1997 on the sitcom _____.

TV Life Real Life

Steven Bochco, creator of the hit shows *L.A. Law* and *NYPD Blue*, also produced what short-lived series that combined music with hard-hitting police drama?

Answers: ❖ Columbo ❖ Bosom Buddies ❖ Roseanne ❖ Cop Rock

Ultimate TV Trivia™

Who on *Gomer Pyle, U.S.M.C.* said, "My old grandmother could do better than that": Col. Edward Gray, Sgt. Vince Carter or Lou-Ann Poovie?

_ _ _ _ _ _ _ _ _ _

On *Benson*, almost all of the interaction between Benson, Gretchen, Katie, Clayton and the Governor took place in what building?

_ _ _ _ _ _ _ _ _ _

Chris Noth plays _____ _____ on *Sex and the City*.

_ _ _ _ _ _ _ _ _ _

Was K.I.T.T., the car used in *Knight Rider*, built from a Trans Am, a Camaro or an IROC?

Answers: ❖ Sgt. Vince Carter ❖ The Governor's Mansion ❖ Mr. Big ❖ A Trans Am

Ultimate TV Trivia ™

Who Said That?

On *Lois and Clark*, a 1990s spin-off of *Superman*, what villain reveals Clark Kent's true identity to Lois Lane?

Where Did It Happen?

On what TV show does Thorny live next door to the Nelsons on Sycamore Road?

Blankety Blanks

The Monkees' member _____ _____ was known for sporting his trademark knit cap.

TV Life Real Life

What wacky talk show host starred in a series of Pepsi® One commercials?

Answers: ✹ Tempus ✹ *The Adventures of Ozzie & Harriet* ✹ Mike Nesmith ✹ Tom Green (*The Tom Green Show*)

Ultimate TV Trivia

Who on *7th Heaven* said, "I like peanut butter, but I don't want it every day!" in response to "But I thought you liked school": Lucy, Mary or Ruthie?

_____ _____ _____ _____

On *Pinky and the Brain*, what do the two animated mice set out to conquer: the world, the universe or the USA?

_____ _____ _____ _____

Academy Award-nominated actor Greg Kinnear was the first host of the cable talk show _____ _____.

_____ _____ _____ _____

TheSmokingGun.com and CrimeLibrary.com are website affiliates of what cable network?

Answers: ❊ Ruthie ❊ The world ❊ *Talk Soup* ❊ Court TV

Ultimate TV Trivia

Who on *Cybill* said, "Oh, Daddy, help me! They're forcing me to me to have fun! Make it stop": Cybill, Zoe or Mary Ann?

In one version of its opening credits, what TV series featured its three main characters walking on the Santa Monica Pier?

Talk show hostess Ricki Lake starred as Tracy Turnblad in the 1988 John Waters comedy, _____.

After Bob Keeshan retired from *Captain Kangaroo*, he was a lobbyist for children's issues and fought for tighter controls against what industry?

Answers: ❖ Zoe ❖ *Three's Company* ❖ *Hairspray* ❖ Tobacco

Collect Spinner Books!

ISBN:
1-57528-907-5

ISBN:
1-57528-915-6

ISBN:
1-57528-916-4

ISBN:
1-57528-906-7

ISBN:
1-57528-905-9

ISBN:
1-57528-909-1

Find these books and more at AreYouGame.com
or your nearest book or toy store.

2030 Harrison Street, San Francisco, CA 94110
1-800-347-4818, www.ugames.com

Enjoy Spinner Books?
Get an original game!

Find these games and more at
or your nearest toy store.